D0708375
WITHDRAWAL

THE HERITAGE OF GREECE AND THE LEGACY OF ROME

E. B. Osborn

DORAN'S MODERN READERS' BOOKSHELF
Edited by Sidney Dark

THE HERITAGE OF GREECE AND THE LEGACY OF ROME
E. B. Osborn

ST. FRANCIS OF ASSISI
Gilbert K. Chesterton

THE STORY OF THE RENAISSANCE
Sidney Dark

HOW TO READ HISTORY
W. Watkin Davies

VICTORIAN POETRY
John Drinkwater

THE POETRY OF ARCHITECTURE
Frank Rutter

ATOMS AND ELECTRONS
J. W. N. Sullivan

EVERYDAY BIOLOGY
J. Arthur Thomson

HOW TO ENJOY LIFE
Sidney Dark

HOW TO ENJOY THE BIBLE
Canon Anthony Deane

Other Volumes in Preparation

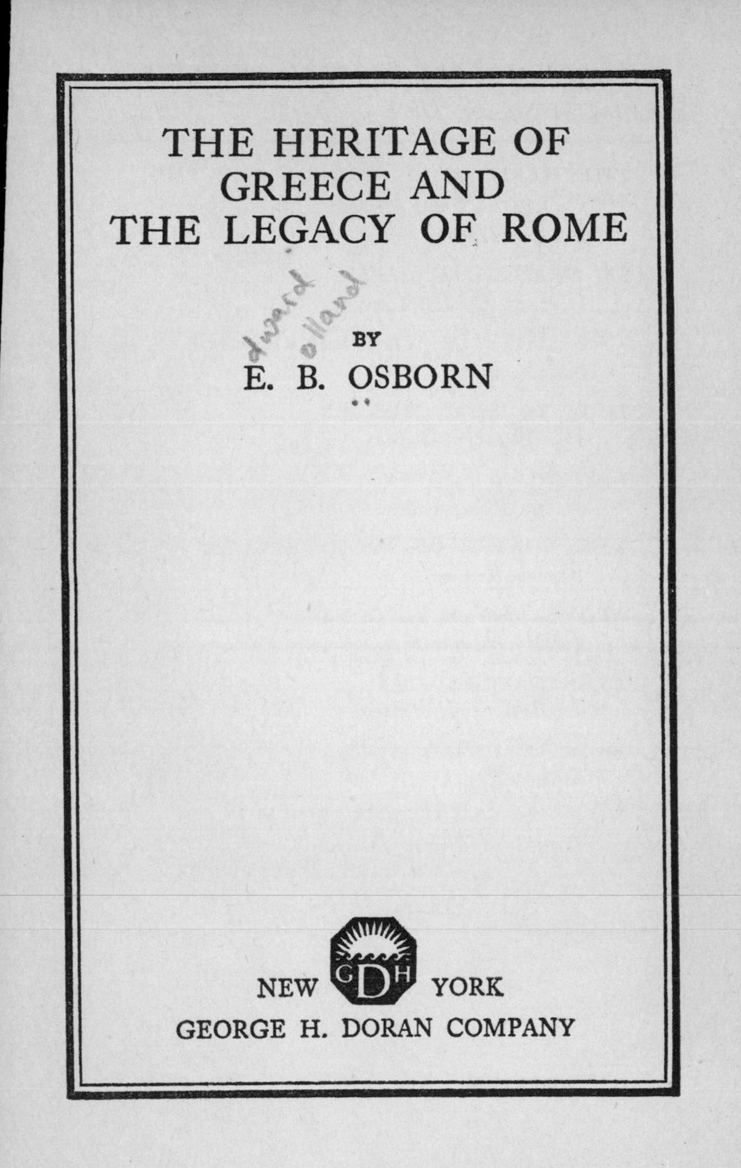

THE HERITAGE OF GREECE AND THE LEGACY OF ROME

BY

E. B. OSBORN

NEW YORK
GEORGE H. DORAN COMPANY

THE HERITAGE OF GREECE AND THE LEGACY OF ROME
— C —
PRINTED IN THE UNITED STATES OF AMERICA

PUBLISHED IN ENGLAND BY HODDER & STOUGHTON
UNDER THE TITLE, "OUR DEBT TO GREECE AND ROME"

Contents

THERE is a famous passage in one of the deeply thoughtful novels of the late Maurice Barrés, which takes the form of a dialogue between a Meadow and a Cloister of four strong stone walls on rising ground near by:—

"I am,"[1] says the Meadow, "the spirit of Earth and of the stocks that spring from Earth; I am liberty; I am inspiration."

And the Cloister answers: "I am established principle. I am authority, the bond with the past; I am an accepted code of human thought; I am the stronghold of man's soul."

But the Meadow speaks again, saying: "I shall trouble that soul of yours. Those who breathe my air are questioning spirits. That he may rest and contemplate, the tiller of the soil comes up to me from his furrowed fields. An instinct draws him to me. I am his first resort; I am an everlasting well-spring."

And again the Cloister speaks that we may hear: "Ye who tarry in the Meadow, come to me with your dreams that I may cleanse them

[1] "La Colline Inspirée."

from worldly dross—bring me your strong enthusiasms that I may direct them aright. . . . We are fellow-products, you and I, of generations past and gone; I am another manifestation of that same spirit. I am enduring stone, the accepted wisdom of the ages, the treasure-house of humanity, the cradle of your early years, the dwelling-place of your Forbears. . . . Come to me—if you would find the footing that cannot fail, a retreat where you can pass your days in calm security, a shelter on whose walls you may write your epitaph."

And so on. It might be a dialogue between ancient Greece, where man used his natural gifts as freely and frankly as Nature meant them to be used, and Rome, which built the lives of men by force into the great fabric of the first world-State. Broadly speaking, Greece was theory and Rome practice. Greece was reason and Rome authority. Greece was self-determination and Rome discipline.

It would be absurd to press this distinction too far. Long before the larger problems of world-governance were to all appearance solved by the establishment of the Roman Empire under Augustus, the history and the civilisation of the Mediterranean world were essentially Graeco-Latin. As early as the fourth century B.C. Rome came into contact with Greek culture in Campania and began to absorb it. The fact that Rome was originally a city-State, like Athens or Sparta, with similar institutions, was a link that was always borne in mind by Greeks and Romans alike. The Greeks never looked upon the Romans as "barbarians," the term they applied to all other races which had a language they could not understand. When in 229 B.C. the Romans first appeared on the eastern shores of the Adriatic, they were at once admitted to membership in the Hellenic games—as though they had been elected to the great Hellenic fellowship as honorary Greeks. In return the Roman Government and influential Romans such as Flamininus adopted a phil-Hellenic policy in their foreign relations. The results of this closer intimacy was seen in the impulse given by Greek models to Latin literature. Greece was conquered in the great explosion of Roman energy after the downfall of Carthage, but in Horace's immortal phrase she "took captive her rude conqueror." So that it is a Graeco-Latin civilisation, which the modern world has inherited as the background, so to speak, of its wonderful mosaic of national cultures.

Yet, as a study of the English language with its many Latin and Greek elements clearly shows, the contributions of the Greek spirit and of the Roman spirit can be distinguished in the way I have indicated. *Theory* is derived from the Greek; *action* and *transaction* from the Latin. *Theology* is Greek; *religion* is Latin. *Poetry* and *philosophy* are Greek; *verse, morality,* and *conduct* are Latin. Nearly all the terminology of the arts and sciences is Greek, and it is a significant fact that modern scientists have built up their innumerable new terms out of Greek elements—*ion* and *electron* are two of their latest inventions. The result is that a modern dictionary is filled with a sort of Neo-Greek language—too often like the French of a menu !—which constitutes a veritable language of the scientific intellect. Some of these terms are distressing hybrids; for example, *sociology* and *Bolshevism*. On the other hand, nearly all our terms of governance are of Latin origin; among them are *state, colony, dominion, municipality, representation, suffrage, election, administration, jurisprudence, justice, legality, Conservative, Liberal, Labour, majority, minority, public, orator, national, rational,* to choose a few out of a great number at random. And you have only to take half-a-dozen pages of an English dictionary to be convinced that there is a real difference between the Greek and the Roman contributions to our modern life—and also to become convinced that our Graeco-Latin heritage is of vital importance, far more important than you had imagined, supposing you had never thought about the matter with a serious intention to get at the whole truth of it. And nowhere will you find this heritage more vitally inwrought than in the Christianity which is still, I feel assured, the chief motive-power in the progress of the various nations onwards and upwards.

The important place occupied by classical studies in our universities and schools is evidence that " the glory that was Greece and the grandeur that was Rome " are living influences in modern life. A century, or even fifty years, ago this argument would have been final. To-day, however, a classical education is disparaged—especially by those who have not had the advantages of it—as pedantic and unpractical. This prejudice, it must be confessed, is justified by the continued prevalence of the antiquated system, which came into vogue in the generations following the Renaissance, whereby a training in Latin and Greek came to mean the study of grammar and philology and the servile copying of classical models. It should, on the contrary, be a study of thought and emotion and the history of mankind as presented in the classical masterpieces. The charge that such a study would still be unpractical —*i. e.* not directly helpful in the earning of a living—could only be used by the arrant materialist who does not know the true intent and scope of education. Its object should be to train the mind, to add adaptability to a pupil's abilities, and to teach him not only to live, but also to live well. And this necessity was thoroughly understood by the ancient Greeks themselves who knew so well the value to a man and to his community of true humanism and, had they seen the horrors of modern industrial monotony, would have approved Mr. G. Sampson's epigram[1] to the effect that "it is the purpose of education not to prepare children *for* their occupations, but to prepare them *against* their occupations."

It is surprising to find scientific workers opposing the teaching of Greek culture. For the Greeks were the pioneers of science, ruthless in the quest of truth, and the most eager of all experimentalists. The ordinary Athenian, even in the day when Athens was impotent for good or evil in world-politics, was always anxious to see, hear, and make new things. He was an adept in all the crafts, but most of all in the craft of living. And contact with his radio-active mind, which would turn with wise wonderment, were he with us to-day, to our telescopes and aeroplanes and other proofs of the soul's new empire over soulless things rather than to our literature and art, is the best reward to be had by the student, whatsoever the subject of his studies. Furthermore, he can teach us the vital nature of the truth expressed in his maxim "know thyself"—that, for example, no social reform can be lasting or truly progressive which is not based on the knowledge of what man is, both as individual and as a member of his community. Character is destiny and character-building the end of all

[1] In "English for the English."

statesmanship—such was the teaching of Socrates, Plato, and Aristotle, and it is a lesson we still have to learn.

But what of Rome? Is she to be considered nothing more than the "great intermediary," who existed to transmit to later ages the message and method of the Greeks? It is true, no doubt, that the Roman lived on a lower plane, so far as spiritual things are concerned, than the Greek in the spring-tide of his works and days. Yet he did what the Greeks could never do; he founded a world-policy, which gave to its citizens the *Pax Romana*, an imperfect yet glorious symbol of the universal peace our souls are even now ensuing. After all, the Roman conquests were not, as Dante thought at first, achieved by the sword alone. Rome was no mere Ashur with a sovereignty won by brute force, leaving nothing behind to solace the spirit of man. In point of fact, looking at tangible instruments, the great city on the Tiber owed more to the plough than to the sword, more to roads than to raids, more to law than to the legionary. She bequeathed to the modern world three great gifts. First of them the vast body of her experience in administrative work, which no statesman can neglect, so full is it of object-lessons for this undisciplined world of ours. Second comes the priceless boon of Roman Law, which is the basis of nearly all modern legal codes and a part of all the rest. Thirdly, there is the

Latin language and its literature, which is for various reasons far more widely known than the greater Greek masterpieces. And it must never be forgotten that the Roman Church is the great unbroken bridge between the modern and the ancient worlds. The Roman Church is the Roman Empire spiritualised—"no other than the ghost of the deceased Roman Empire sitting crowned upon the grave thereof," according to the immortal metaphor of Hobbes of Malmesbury. "The history of that Church," wrote Macaulay, "joins together the two great ages of human civilisation. No other institution is left standing which carries the mind back to the times when the smoke of sacrifice rose from the Pantheon and when camelopards and tigers bounded in the Flavian Amphitheatre." So our Roman heritage, if it does not appeal to the imagination as poignantly as our legacy from Greece, is yet a mighty thing and one to be grateful for. Let us go down into the everlasting Meadow, afterwards visiting the Cloister, a sentinel in stone, on her eternal hill.

Chapter II *The Greek Spirit*

I

In all the works and days of man the spirit counts for more than the letter. The idea or ideal is the vital thing—not the imperfect attempts to express it in poetry or prose, in statuary or painting, in the action of drama, in a political constitution, in religious ceremonial. It is especially so in the case of Greek achievement. Such tangible results of it as we have inherited are magnificent and momentous, though little more than the wreckage of time and far indeed from representing " the glory that was Greece " at the epoch when Athens reached the height of her prosperity under the wise leadership of the far-sighted Pericles. Even those who know nothing and care less about the object-lessons of antiquity cannot help being impressed by all these amazing fragments. Nobody can see the great temple of the Parthenon brooding in its haggard, time-worn beauty on the height above modern Athens without feeling a lump in his throat. I have heard quite illiterate visitors to the British Museum cry out in surprise at their first sight of the Greek statuary there, the huge stolen fragments known as the Elgin marbles being particularly awe-inspiring. And those who read the masterpieces of Greek literature for the first time, even in translations, feel as Keats did when he opened Chapman's Homer. They are visited by an "aching wonderment" (to quote a phrase I heard from a working man turned student) as they voyage through the unknown Pacific of letters—the epics of Homer; the plays of Æschylus, Sophocles, and Euripides; the histories of Herodotus, Thucydides, Polybius; the odes of Pindar; the dialogues of Plato and Aristotle's treatises; and the little living pictures of life in the Greek world which make up the Palatine Anthology. Familiarity has in some cases bred forgetfulness of the Greek origin of books in constant use to-day. Plain people, with the "practical man's" contempt for so-called dead languages, are apt to be quite startled when reminded that our New Testament is a translation from the Greek, and that not only the geometry of Euclid, but also all elementary mathematics, are derived from Greek sources. Great are the relics we possess of Greek achievement, but greater still is the spirit which inspired them and of which, all said and done, they were in their pristine completeness but imperfect realisations. For it was this spirit, not the tangible expressions of it such as books and statues, which caused that great awakening of the human intellect known as the Renaissance and so brought into being the mobile modern world out of the fixed mediæval order—as a butterfly flying in the sunshine is evolved from a chrysalis attached to the underside of a cabbage leaf. The Greek spirit, recovered by the interpretation of its works, proved a noble contagion. It taught men to trust their intelligence and imagination once more, to question the authority of mediæval theologians and philosophers, and to steep themselves again in Nature. It persuaded them to see the world as it is and to enjoy it—not to make life a period of penances undertaken in the hope of winning a place in a feudal Heaven. It restored a long-lost freedom to the minds of men, and to their "miserable bodies" the right, denied by theologians for more than a thousand years, to enjoy all the natural pleasures, above all the passion that makes man and woman one flesh. Not only was this revival of the Greek spirit the chief cause of the Renaissance, but it also worked below the obvious surface of historical events as a most important factor in the making of the Reformation.

In the great civilisations of the Orient intellectual as well as religious life was controlled by a sacerdotal caste, which preserved from all innovations a sacred tradition enshrined in a sacred book. The Greeks had many temples—but no Church which dictated what men should believe in from an unassailable fortress of authority. Homer was their Bible in a sense, but little more sanctity was attached to texts from it than we attach to quotations from Shakespeare. The consequences of the freedom from a controlling priesthood of any kind were twofold. In the first place, the Greeks could, and did, discuss theological topics with almost complete freedom so long as they did not combine in a group to oppose some religious observance favoured by the State. Denying the existence of Pallas Athene would have been severely punished, no doubt, by the Athenian authorities. But, talking among your friends, you could have poked scandalous fun at the other gods and goddesses with absolute impunity. As for the oracles of Delphi, though received with outward respect, they carried as much or as little weight with the average citizen as the pronouncements on public matters of, say, the Bishop of London do to-day with Londoners. Heresy hunts were unknown; the burning alive of heretics was an act of religious faith as yet undreamed of. Secondly, and on the other hand, poets and philosophers were much more strictly called to account for their moral sentiments than is the case in modern times. Thus Euripides was bitterly attacked for making one of his characters say: "My tongue has sworn, my mind has not taken the oath." Had he been a Greek dramatist, Shakespeare would probably have been taken to task for putting into the mouths of his personages such irreconcilable sentiments as Hamlet's :—

> "There's a divinity that shapes our ends,"

and Gloucester's frenzied railing at destiny :—

> "As flies to wanton boys, are we to the gods;
> They kill us for their sport."

This close and intelligent scrutiny of the religious and moral tendencies of poems, plays, and philosophies compelled the writers thereof to take their tasks very seriously indeed, and they were quite incapable of the worst faults of irresponsible modern authors—for example, the fleshliness of certain English poets and the cheap cynicism of several English playwrights.

The debt we owe to ancient Greece for the boon of the Greek spirit, blowing like a fresh, cool, ozone-laden sea-breeze into the dark and stagnant atmosphere of man's mediæval prison-house, is quite incalculable. And there have been earlier and later manifestations of its influence than Renaissance and Reformation in the larger affairs of the Western world. Whenever we find in the Middle Ages a fresh and courageous mind at work, thinking for itself logically rather than theologically, investigation shows that some knowledge of Greek literature was involved. It was so with Duns Scotus and other Irish teachers (the *Scoti* were, of course, the Celtic Irish) whose intellectual power and European reputation were largely due to the fact that, when the barbarian invasions had overwhelmed

Continental Europe and swept away the vestiges of Greek learning, that treasure of the soul still existed in an Ireland that was as yet solitary and unravaged. Few and far-separated in space and time were these bright sparks of the Greek spirit. Outside the circuit of Christendom, however, the light and warmth of the intellectual "Greek fire" could always be felt. In the Byzantine Empire it glowed sombrely until the fall of Constantinople (Byzantium was originally a city-State whose friendship was always cultivated by ancient Athens) sent the burning embers of Greek literature and art flying broadcast through Western Europe. Then the Islamic culture, which passed along the shores of the Mediterranean to Spain, where it blossomed to fruition under the Moorish dispensation, was plenarily inspired by the Greek spirit. In the case of Islam, as in that of Rome, the conquered led the conquerors captive; the Greek learning of the Hellenised lands and cities taken by the followers of Mahomet was for centuries a victorious inspiration. And when, by way of Arabic translations, translated again into mediæval Latin, the works of Aristotle became known in Christendom, they were made the intellectual foundations of a vast reconstruction of Christian theology, as impressive in its way as the greatest and most elaborate of the historic cathedrals.

Such were the chief pre-Renaissance examples

of the creative influence of the Greek spirit, even when fitfully and remotely felt. But there has been a modern instance of the kind. Many of the principal actors in the tremendous drama of the French Revolution were directly or indirectly inspired by the ideals of Freedom and Justice which are the fruit of the Greek spirit, as applied to political theory, and penetrate the whole body of Greek thought, and were actually realised in some of the Greek city-States. They saw themselves as tyrannicides after the pattern of Harmodius and Aristogeiton; some of them took Greek names. Both the incitement to the Revolutionary spirit and the appropriate antidote to the same are to be found in the history of the Peloponnesian War (in which the great struggle between the Athenian Empire and Sparta with her Allies were complicated by an epidemic of class-warfare); and the account by Thucydides of the "Terror" in Corcyra, with the moral he draws from it, is a salutary warning to every time and clime of what must happen when partisans ignore the dictates of morality to achieve political ends. "When men are retaliating upon others," says Thucydides, "they are reckless of the future, and do not hesitate to annul those common laws of humanity to which every individual trusts for his own hope of deliverance, should he ever be overtaken by calamity; they forget that in their own hour of need they will look for the help of these laws in vain." The actions of "Reds" and of "Whites," as we have seen them in modern revolutions and counter-revolutions, are alike repugnant to the Greek spirit, which loathed excess and extremists and made "Nothing Too Much" its guiding maxim in all the arts, but especially in the great art of living with one's fellow-men.

Enough has been said to show how profoundly the stream of tendencies with its tides of thought called European history has been affected by the undying spirit of the Helles that has been. Let us complete this survey by quoting a few sentences by Professor Gilbert Murray, the most accomplished Greek scholar of this or perhaps any other age, and a master of English, furthermore, whose English verse translations have revitalised our conception of ancient Greek drama :—

"There is a profound rule of art, bidding a man in the midst of all his study of various styles or his pursuit of his own peculiar imaginations, from time to time *se retremper dans la nature*—to steep himself again in Nature. And in something the same way it seems as if the world ought from time to time to steep itself again in Hellenism : that is, it ought, amid all the varying affectations and extravagances and changes of conventions in art and letters, to have some careful regard for those which arose when men first awoke to the meaning of truth and beauty and saw the world freely as a new thing."

And, as shall be shown, even the so-called practical man, whether he be politician or man of business or scientific worker, will gain by bathing his soul in the day-spring of spirituality that was struck out of the bed-rock of human nature in the lower part of the Balkan Peninsula, in a territory which is small and poverty-stricken to modern ideas, during the fifth century before Christ.

II

But how is the Greek spirit to be defined? In point of fact, it is more easily felt than defined. Still, we shall not go far astray if our definition takes the form of a reasoned catalogue of its chief attributes:—Truth-seeking; Beauty; Sanity; Simplicity; and Freshness or, if you will, Youngness.

(1) Truth-seeking is a characteristic of all Greek science, art, and literature. No doubt the Greeks told as many lies in their every-day life as any other race, ancient or modern; indeed some of their sophists (equivalents of the modern journalist in many respects) made the deceiving of masses of men a fine art. But in their contemplation of the world without and the world within—the visible universe and the heart of man—the Greek thinkers lived up to the saying of Anaxagoras when asked for what purpose he was brought into the world: "To meditate on

the works of Nature." They tried to see things as they are, not as they might or ought to be. They could not, of course, escape the consequences of the habit of self-seeking, deeply ingrained in human nature, which is defined in our familiar quotation: "The wish is father to the thought." But they did their best to fight against personal predilections and prejudices, to eliminate the personal equation, to put themselves and their lives into a just perspective. They courageously cultivated that disinterestedness which is the chief quality of the scientific investigator of to-day. We get striking instances of this faculty of dispassionate detachment in the Greek historians, who were singularly free from the modern historian's weakness for taking sides. The classic instance is the account by Thucydides of the incident in the Peloponnesian War which brought about his disgrace, downfall, and long exile from the city he must have loved with the mingled, all-engrossing, heart-rending passion one feels for an unfaithful mistress. Brasidas, the Spartan general, was anxious to take Amphipolis, an Athenian colony on the Struma and a place of considerable strategic importance. Thucydides was then at Thasos, half a day's voyage away. Here is what we are told of the affair:—

"As soon as Thucydides heard the news about Brasidas, he sailed quickly to Amphipolis . . . so as to garrison it, if possible, before it capitulated, or at any rate to occupy Eion (its sea-port). Meanwhile Brasidas, fearing the arrival of the Athenian fleet at Thasos and hearing that Thucydides . . . was one of the leading men of the country, did his utmost to get possession of the city, before he arrived. So he offered easy terms. . . . These terms were accepted and the city was surrendered to him. On the evening of the same day Thucydides and his ships sailed into Eion, but not until Brasidas had taken possession of Amphipolis; another night, and he would have seized Eion."

It is impossible to believe that any modern general would thus describe an affair which wrecked his professional career. We should expect a chapter—perhaps a whole volume—of explanation and self-justification. But Thucydides recognises the fact that he and the disaster which broke him are but minute matters, after all, in comparison with the tremendous tragedy which ended in the destruction of the Syracusan expeditionary force and the delayed, but inevitable, fall of the Athenian Empire. Again, the Greek writers were incapable of that falsification of values which is the ruling vice of modern novelists, whether they be specialists in the happy ending or, like Mr. Thomas Hardy, load the dice against the heroes and heroines of their dismal dramas. They wrote of life as it is, of men and women as they knew them, and they did so without the struggle to be veracious which is a characteristic of modern writers who call themselves realists—a struggle which invariably pushes them towards the precipices of a pessimism unwarranted by the facts!

(2) The Beauty, which is also a characteristic of all Greek art, is perhaps too naked and unadorned for the modern world. The subtleties of it are necessarily lost in the best translations of Greek poetry, which, if they be poetical, are compelled to give us touches of English beauty, by no means the same thing. The elements of beauty, which are lost in the process of translation, are of two kinds. First, those which arise out of the very nature of the Greek language which can express the finest shades of thought or emotion with an easy grace impossible in English, Latin, or even French. Secondly, there are the felicities that are the reward of consummate technique—of an ear for the music of words that is for us an alien thing, not to be reproduced on our own modern instruments of expression. Nevertheless we can appreciate what Newman called " the vivid exactness and sad earnestness " of the best Greek writing, and also the strategic art, so to speak, of such a verse-form as the Homeric hexameter which so many poets have tried to adapt into English with scant success. Now and again a true hexameter is evolved as in A. H. Clough's line :—

> "Dangerous Corrievechan where roads are unknown to
> Loch Nevish,"

but as a general rule the English imitation, as may be seen from a study of Longfellow's *Evangeline*, is a wooden and splay-footed affair in comparison with the infinitely-varying Homeric hexameter. Much of the beauty of Greek literature is incommunicable—not fully comprehended, it may be, by the best Greek scholars—and yet that which *can* be appreciated is sufficient to carry away the soul of a Keats into an ecstasy of wonderment. The beauty of a Greek statue, again, is not easily appreciated by the admirers of Rodin or Epstein. It is all a beauty of structure, without ornament; and it is apt to appear "uninteresting" to those who find in it nothing of the strangeness which Bacon thought to be a part of all excellent beauty, a ruling which no Greek critic would have accepted. Yet a careful study will enable you to recognise the austere and stately loveliness of such a work of art (one that you can *live* with) and will bring you in the end to the wisdom which endures for ever in the famous lines of Keats inspired by the sight of a Greek vase :—

> "Beauty is truth, truth beauty—that is all
> Ye know on earth and all ye need to know."

(3) The Sanity of all Greek art is the counterpart of moderation (*Sophrosyne*) in the moral

sphere. The Greek artist did not care for the abnormal; he did not depict a survival of the unfittest, physically or spiritually considered, or choose a grotesque ruin such as "La Vieille Héaulmière" of Rodin's for the subject of a statue. He was quite free from the Puritanical, or anti-Puritanical, prejudices which drive modern writers into excess in one direction or the other. He saw life and he saw it whole, and expressed what he saw in marble or his singularly plastic language without losing his temper or his temperament.

(4) Simplicity is another note of all Greek art. Like the simple life, however, this simplicity is the last term in a long series of experiments in pruning away all distractions. Study a Greek bas-relief, for example, and you will find that its simplicity—perhaps inevitableness would be the better term—is the outcome of nice adjustments all tending to create the same impression in the mind of the observer. In literature you need only compare a Greek epitaph from the Palatine Anthology with any well-known *in memoriam* poem in English to see how much the fine things left unsaid strengthen your impression of a single dominating emotion of sorrow. Tennyson's *In Memoriam* or Shelley's *Adonais* would have suggested to a Greek the spectacle of a wounded man fingering his wound and finding an un-Greek pleasure in each titillating pain.

The Greeks knew far better than we do the tremendous power of reticence in any work of art which, to be thoroughly effective, must leave comment to the observer's imagination.

(5) Finally, there is the quality—definitely felt, not easily defined—of Freshness or Youngness. There is a bloom on the Greek masterpieces which writers of to-day, knowing that everything has been said before and that they are adding yet another to millions of existing books, cannot hope to impress on their own work. In the age when Athens was the capital of the world's culture all things seemed possible to the adventurous spirit, and the intellectual atmosphere was full of the ozone of hopefulness. Now we know too well, alas! that all we can look forward to is a closer approach, century by century, to the realisation of our ideals—provided, of course, the civilisation we have so laboriously won is not destroyed by our own fanatical folly. To read the Greek masterpieces, then, is to regain in some measure the first rapture of hopefulness and to be young again for certain immortal moments.

THE story of the rise, decline, and fall of States and the political lessons conveyed have never been more finely, more intelligently, expressed than by the great Greek historians. To-day there is a tendency to regard the political experience of the Greek States as of little use to modern nations because (1) they were small in extent and population, and (2) much of the hard, joyless work was done by slave labour. But a laboratory experiment, though on a very small scale, may give most helpful information to those engaged in large operations, and the slaves in ancient communities may be taken as a kind of " robots "—mechanical persons performing the functions of modern machinery. The differences in question must, however, always be taken into account and the absurdity avoided of basing forecasts of the failure of modern democracy on sentences from a Greek historian or philosopher. The Greeks themselves would have scoffed at such foolish reasoning, and the notion of a classical education based on the microscopic study of ancient languages, no longer spoken, would have seemed to them ridiculous in the extreme, for they themselves learnt no language save their own and thought it sufficient for all purposes of self-culture. Again, the differences of outlook on internal and external affairs which distinguish the Greek from a modern Englishman or Frenchman must always be duly considered. As regards the internal affairs of his State, the Greek politician entirely lacked the modern conception of individual liberty; when a citizen, as Thucydides said of the typical Athenian, "spent his body, as a mere external tool, in the service of his city and counted his intellect as most surely his own when employed on her behalf," he seemed to the Greek historians and philosophers to be completely fulfilling his duty to his neighbour and to himself. The distinction between the domain of the individual's conscience and the political sphere would have seemed meaningless to the subtlest of Greek thinkers. Religious objections to any course of action prescribed by the State—*e. g.* conscientious scruples about military service—would have been looked upon by the average Athenian as sheer imbecility; for Athens and the goddess Athena were to him practically identical. Again, the whole mass of industrial problems, which form the greater part of modern politics, were practically non-existent for the citizen of Athens or Sparta, Thebes or Corinth. Had they been presented to any Greek philosopher he would probably have suggested the enslavement of the workers as the only practicable solution. Again, foreign policy in our sense of the term is a matter on which the ancient Greek writers can give us no useful counsel. Humanity as a whole was a conception which never entered their heads, for they divided human beings into two sections—Greeks and Barbarians—and the all-engrossing duty of the former was to preserve the little oasis of Greek civilisation from the attacks of the latter, whose manners and customs were misunderstood and despised as beast-like in the main. The business of forming alliances and counter-alliances was, of course, a matter of vital importance to the statesmen of the Greek city-States. But their statecraft, theoretical and applied, is not prolific in object-lessons for those who are concerned with the infinitely complex relations subsisting between the great communities, several of them world-States and all interested in world-politics, which occupy this self-conscious planet to-day.

Within the limitations indicated above, however, there is much to be learnt from a study of Greek history. After all the ancient Greeks were much more like than unlike ourselves; indeed there is an extraordinarily close resemblance, both social and political, between the English of to-day and the Athenians when they were the citizens of an Empire based on sea-power like our own. The three greatest Greek historians—Herodotus, Thucydides, and Xenophon—were all men of action and travellers, and their books show us men as they are (not as they might be or ought to be) faced by the tremendous crises which bring out the points of strength and the weaknesses that are constant terms in human nature. The attributes of the crowd are invariable in all times and climes, it would seem, and all three are experts in crowd psychology. As stories only, often stranger than fiction, their books would deserve to be immortal; for the reading of them cleanses the mind of meanness and self-seeking (the *katharsis* which is the purpose of all great tragedy) and at the same time leaves us our pride in man's unconquerable soul. What, for example, could be more moving—and more appealing to us who but lately escaped the possibility of a similar fate—than the account by Thucydides of the last fatal defeat of the Athenian Expeditionary Force in the Syracusan Bay. "Others too," said the Athenian General, the pious and good Nicias, on that tremendous occasion, "having done what men may, have borne what men must." "This is the very burden of life," wrote the late Andrew Lang, taking that sad sentence for his text, "and the last word of tragedy. For now all is vain: courage, wisdom, piety, the bravery of Lamarchus, the goodness of Nicias, the brilliance of Alcibiades are all expended, all wasted, nothing of that brave venture abides, except torture, defeat, and death.

No play nor poem is so moving as this ruin of a people; no modern story can stir us, with all its eloquence, like the brief gravity of this ancient history. Nor can we find, at the last, any wisdom more wise than that which bids us do what men may and bear what men must. Such are the lessons of the Greeks, of the people who tried all things, in the morning of the world, and who still speak to us of what they tried in words which are the sum of human gaiety and gloom, of grief and triumph, hope and despair. The world, since that day, has but followed in the same round, which only seems new: has only made the same experiments, and failed with the same failure, but less gallantly and gloriously."

HERODOTUS (484–425 B.C.)

Wordsworth thought the "History" (meaning "inquiry") of Herodotus the most interesting and instructive book, next to the Bible, which has ever been written. His object was "that the great and wonderful deeds done by Greeks and Persians should not lack renown." It is characteristic of the "Father of History" that he does not pour obloquy on the enemies of his race and country or refuse to give them praise when they deserve it for valour and chivalrous forbearance. An Ionian by birth, he wrote in an Ionian dialect. He was an exile from his native city, Halicarnassus, and he travelled far and wide

—northward to the Crimea, southward to Assouan, eastward to Persia, and westward to Sicily—before settling down, at any rate to the extent of spending his later years between Athens and Thurii in Italy, a colony which he had helped to found. He did not know the languages of the many countries through which he travelled, and he had something of the gullibility of a tourist. However, he explains that he thinks himself bound to put down what he hears, but not to believe it all, which does not excuse him for relating conversations he could not possibly have overheard. The imaginary speech, by the way, is a device much used by all Greek historians and by the Roman writers who imitated them. It is not meant to be taken as actually spoken, but as a convenient method of summarising a statesman's or general's plans and political motives. The Greek historians wrote like the dramatists and authors of epics or idylls, leaving persons and episodes to speak for themselves and not interpolating comments, as is the modern custom, or trying to re-create the atmosphere of the time and place. If he had done his work in the manner of a modern historian in his study, he would have begun with the Minoan civilisation (of which many rumours must have survived, though Knossos was a buried city, haunted by evil spirits) and shown his readers that his Greece was but the last term (for him) of many centuries of development. All is fish that comes to the net of his observant eye, whether fact or fancy, and the result is that his book is full of varied interest and stirring movement. The scientific historian of to-day, by reducing his book to a sort of dust-heap of circumstance and carefully sifting it, has been able to find a vast deal of the gold of exact historical truth in Herodotus and so to justify to some extent the boast that we know more about the making of Greece than the Greeks ever knew. Herodotus had one very great merit as an historian; he was instinctively aware, being the Odysseus of his craft, that geography is the skeleton of history, so to speak. Finally, he has the priceless gift of story-telling—had he lived to-day, he must have been a " best seller "—and he enthrals and thrills the reader, whether he is telling a fairy tale or dealing with the romance of warfare. His story of the war with Persia is uncritical from the point of view of a modern military historian; for example, he greatly exaggerates the Persian forces which, as Delbrück has shown, were almost certainly less numerous than those of the allied Greeks. But commissariat questions and the wastage of forces in the field were not subjects which he worried about. His object was to write a drama showing how the overweening and insolent confidence (*hubris*) of the Persian King brought about the ruin of his land and sea forces.

Thucydides (455–399 B.C.)

There can be no doubt whatever that Thucydides was one of the greatest men who ever lived. I have a vivid recollection of seeing his portrait-bust at Holkham Hall in Norfolk, which gives a shock of surprise even to those who come prepared for the sight of it, so powerful and defiant is the whole expression of the proudly-erect head. Here is the effigy, you say to yourself, of one who was stronger than the marble itself; great in his intelligence, as the fine, high brow and deep-receding temples plainly show, but greater still in the unbreakable will-power, which could outface the catastrophe that had befallen his unkind and ungrateful, yet passionately loved, Athens. The bust statue of Demosthenes shows us one who was a weakling in comparison. Thucydides was related to some of the greatest Athenian families, and he was sent into exile in 424 B.C. because he failed, when commanding the Athenian fleet, to prevent the loss of Amphipolis, a town of great strategic importance. The incident, which throws a beam of light on the Greek disinterestedness in truth-seeking, has been touched on in an earlier chapter. He was not allowed to return to Athens until 404 B.C., when the Peloponnesian war ended in the utter defeat of the Athenian Empire, and he seems to have travelled about during the twenty years of his banishment, observing the war from the standpoint of Athens' enemies. Had he not been exiled, we might never have had his incomparable history.

As a historian, his sole aim is truth. "I have described nothing," he says when explaining his method, "but what I either saw myself or learned from others of whom I made the most careful and particular inquiry." He goes on to tell us that his task was very laborious, because eye-witnesses gave different accounts of the same occurrence, being misled by interest in the fortunes of one side or the other. His style is often artificial and involved when he is not relating things that happened; he struggles, one feels, to express fully, and with precision, the results of his profound reflections. A schoolmaster of my acquaintance once compared his intricate style with that of Henry James, who, like him, was never content with the obvious or superficial comment on human motives. He is the first scientific historian, and I cannot think of any modern writer of history who is his equal in impartiality and the disinterested weighing of available evidence. Did we not know who and what he was, we could not tell from his narrative whether he was an Athenian or a Spartan. Yet he feels in his heart's core the tragic significance of the great drama of the war between the Athenian Empire and the league of rival States with Sparta at its head—a war which, like that between the Allies and the Central European Powers, was also a contest between forms of governance, democracy and oligarchy. There are two threads of inquiry which cross and re-cross in his narrative of the great struggle—great in the intense preoccupation of the belligerents, though the city-States allied on either side were petty in wealth and population according to modern ideas, and the theatre of amphibious warfare narrow and restricted. First, there is the story of the destruction of the Athenian Empire by Sparta and her allies; secondly, there is the degeneration of the Empire itself from a liberal democracy, such as the great-souled Pericles wished it to remain, into a tyranny, which was mob-driven and as ruthless in its *real-politik* as Germany under its war-lords, and in the end self-destroyed by attempting a colossal adventure beyond its means in men and treasure. He also shows—a third point which brings home to us the resemblance of the Peloponnesian war in its broad outline to the recent world-struggle—how the struggle between the Athenian and Spartan leagues was complicated and made absolutely ruinous to Greece by a truceless class-warfare, the worst of all calamities that can befall mankind.

Furthermore, he proves himself one of the greatest scientific sociologists that ever lived. He has anticipated in his opening chapters all the sciences that are the handmaids of history. His account of the evolution of Greek society from the earliest times to his own era is a masterly achievement. Little wonder that Freeman could say of him: "There is hardly a problem in the science of government which the statesman will not find handled, if not solved, in the pages of this universal master." He was always a man of the world, moreover; he knew men and never forgot that institutions are man-made things. By common consent he is the greatest of all historians, and the oft-quoted saying that his history—which ends in a broken sentence, in 411 B.C. when the fate of Athens was already clearly indicated—could be printed in the space of a single issue of *The Times* must not blind us to the fact that it is worth all the mass of modern journalism for the last century.

Here is an excerpt which may persuade the reader to study this master of human nature and statecraft in one of the several good translations which now exist. It is a passage from the Funeral Oration of Pericles, delivered in 431 B.C., which defines the Athenian ideals of patriotism and citizenship, and shows how closely akin the Athenian was to the modern Englishman; which is the reason why I give it.

"My first words shall be for our ancestors; it is both just to them and seemly that on an occasion such as this our tribute of memory should be paid them. For, dwelling always in this country, generation after generation in unchanging and unbroken succession, they have handed it down to us free by their exertions. So they are worthy of our praises; and still more so are our fathers. For they enlarged the ancestral patrimony by the Empire which we hold to-day and delivered it, not without labour, into the hands of our own generation; while it is we ourselves, those of us who are now in middle life, who consolidated our power throughout the greater part of the Empire and secured the city's complete independence both in war and peace. Of the battles which we and our fathers fought, whether in the winning of our power abroad or in bravely withstanding the warfare of foreigner or Greek at home, I do not wish to say more: they are too familiar to you all. I wish rather to set forth the spirit in which we faced them, and the constitution and manners with which we rose to greatness, and to pass from them to the dead.

"Our government is not copied from those of our neighbours: we are an example to them rather than they to us. Our constitution is named a democracy, because it is in the hands not of the few but of the many. But our laws secure equal justice for all in their private disputes, and our public opinion welcomes and honours talent in every branch of achievement, not for any sectional reason but on grounds of excellence alone. And as we give free play to all in our public life, so we carry the same spirit into our daily relations with one another. We have no black ooks or angry words for our neighbour if he enjoys himself in his own way, and we abstain from the little acts of churlishness which, though they leave no mark, yet cause annoyance to whoso notes them. Open and friendly in our private intercourse, in our public acts we keep strictly within the control of the law. We acknowledge the restraint of reverence; we are obedient to those in authority, and to the laws, more especially to those which offer protection to the oppressed and those unwritten ordinances whose transgression brings admitted shame. Yet ours is no workaday city only. No other provides so many recreations for the spirit—games and sacrifices all the year round, and beauty in our public buildings to cheer the heart and delight the eye day by day.

"Our military training, too, is different from our opponents'. The gates of our city are flung open to the world. We practise no periodical deportations, nor do we prevent our visitors from observing or discovering what an enemy might usefully apply to his own purposes. For our trust is not in the devices of material equipment, but in our own good spirits for battle.

"So too with education. They toil from early boyhood in a laborious pursuit after courage, while we, free to live and wander as we please, march out none the less to face the self-same dangers. Indeed, if we choose to face danger with an easy mind rather than after a rigorous training, and to trust rather in native manliness than in State-made courage, the advantage lies with us; for we are spared all the weariness of practising for future hardships, and when we find ourselves amongst them we are as brave as our plodding rivals. Here as elsewhere, then, the city sets an example which is deserving of admiration. We are lovers of beauty without extravagance, and lovers of wisdom without unmanliness. Wealth to us is not mere means of display but an opportunity for achievement; and poverty we think it no disgrace to acknowledge, but a real degradation to make no effort to overcome. Our citizens attend both to public and private duties, and do not allow absorption in their own various affairs to interfere with their knowledge of the city's. We differ from other States in regarding the man who holds aloof from public life not as 'quiet' but as useless; we decide or debate, carefully and in person, all matters of policy, holding, not that words and deeds go ill together, but that acts are foredoomed to failure when undertaken undiscussed. For we are noted for being at once most adventurous in action and most reflective beforehand. Other men are bold in ignorance, while reflection will stop their onset. But the bravest are surely those who have the clearest vision of what is before them, glory and danger alike, and yet notwithstanding go out to meet it. In a word I claim that our city as a whole is an education to Greece, and that her members yield to none, man by man, for independence of spirit, many-sidedness of attainment, and complete self-reliance in limbs and brain."

Xenophon (426–359 B.C.)

There is no Greek writer, I think, quite so English as Xenophon, soldier and sportsman and man of letters, whose plain, natural, unaffected style of writing always has the charm of perfect clearness and literary good breeding. He is a type which has perhaps been more common in England than in any other country, ancient or modern; the kindly gentleman, with experience of war in his young days, who combines the open-air life with intellectual interests. He had known Socrates and loved and admired him, and we learn from him how that wonderful man could influence young men without the reckless brilliance of an Alcibiades or the poetical and intellectual power of a Plato. Though not a profound historian, like Thucydides, he has a reverence for the truth, the whole truth, and nothing but the truth, and his "Hellenica" is an invaluable source of information about the history of Greece. His books on Hunting and the Education of Cyrus are priceless jewels of their kind, for they bring us into sympathetic touch with the social life of more than two thousand years ago. Moreover, he wrote a work on household management, which Ruskin made the basis, as he confesses, of his humanised economics. His books, if they do not rank as the greatest literature, give us a living picture of a Greek gentleman, competent and keen and making the best of himself and his friends and the varied world about him. It is a pity that his "Anabasis" has been no more than a grammar-grind for the vast majority of boys for whom a so-called classical education is the pedagogue's substitute for humanism.

The " Anabasis " is the story of an astounding military adventure, which first revealed to the Greeks the cumbrous weakness and seizable wealth of the much-dreaded Persian Empire. Once its weakness was known, the conquests of Alexander the Great and the Hellenisation of the East which followed were inevitable. Late in the summer of 401 B.C. a force of 10,000 Greek mercenaries was in a very tight corner indeed in the plains of Mesopotamia near the vast city of Babylon, then the most populous metropolis in the world. Cyrus, their leader, who was attempting to wrest the throne from his elder brother, had fallen in a battle which had been won to all intents and purposes by his valiant mercenaries. Their generals had been entrapped and murdered, and near at hand was a huge Persian army. There was nothing to do but try to reach the Black Sea by following the Tigris. Xenophon and Cheirisophus, a Spartan, were chosen as leaders, and they led the army safely to the sea in spite of continual fighting, terrible hardships in the mountain snows, and the ever-recurring difficulties of procuring food. It was a wonderful feat of arms, and Xenophon describes it with soldierly vivacity —we hear all the humours of the march, including the little chaffing-matches between the Athenian and the Spartan leader. And as regards the behaviour of the army, the combination of military precision with the reflecting obedience of citizens, who elect their generals, "confers" (to use Grote's words) " immortal distinction on the Hellenic character."

These three great historians cover but a small part of the long course of Greek history, which begins in the pre-Homeric days with the arrival of migrants from Central Europe and does not really end until the fall of the Byzantine Empire. The later stages of this continuous and complex story are all illuminated by Greek historians. Polybius, who was one of the greatest of military historians, with a perfect understanding of large political issues, is as Greek as the three whose merits have been analysed at length. It is impossible to distinguish, later on, between Greek and Roman history. Bolshevism, as the story of Aristonikos and his outlaw followers shows, might be included in the list of Greek political errors. The great era of class-wars (tyrannical " big business," followed by Bolshevism and Napoleonism) was 146–31 B.C. The Greek historian of personalities, Greek and Roman, appears in Plutarch, one of the most entrancing of writers, with an eye for the anecdote that depicts a character in a lightning-flash, and both St. Paul and Marcus Aurelius deliver their messages of hope or despair not only in the Greek language, but also in the Greek manner. It is impossible to doubt that modern civilisations—nay, even the revolutionary schemes which aim at destroying it—have a Græco-Roman basis.

Chapter IV — Greek Science

ALL our sciences, like the names of them, are of Greek origin. Indeed it would be possible to maintain the thesis that this part of our debt to ancient Greece is one of more consequence than all the masterpieces of literature and art she has bequeathed to us. As men possessed of an insatiable love of truth-seeking, a noble madness for seeing things as they are and not as they might be or ought to be, Euclid, Aristotle (as biologist), and Hippocrates (the wise physician) might be rated as more typically Greek than Homer, Sophocles, and Thucydides. The latter have given us undying pictures of men and cities, of human exaltations and agonies which even to-day help us to understand the mysteries of human nature, for even the people of the far-off Homeric Age were more like than unlike ourselves. But the work of the former is indispensable in a higher degree, seeing that it is actually part of the very foundation of the knowledge by, in, and for which the modern world goes on living.

I

The rudiments of Greek mathematics came from the Egyptians and Babylonians. Thales

(624–547 B.C.), with whom Greek geometry and astronomy begin, travelled in Egypt and learnt the methods used there for measuring areas of land and the contents of vessels of various shapes. He and Pythagoras, who also visited Egypt and is said to have become initiated into the temple rites there, not out of religious enthusiasm, but so as not to miss any scrap of knowledge worth having, had a very important advantage over the Egyptians. They were not hampered in turning what they found to good account by an organised and dominating priestly caste which always has a tendency to see mystical meanings in certain numbers (huge tomes were written on such topics in the Middle Ages) and is apt to cover up scientific results in religious ordinances. They were able to give their reasoning powers fair play and so to make generalisations. Thus the Egyptians knew that a triangle with its sides in the ratio of 3, 4, and 5 has a right angle opposite the longest side and used this fact as a means of drawing a right angle. But they never got beyond the *particular case*—they never considered the *general property* of right-angled triangles established by Euclid (Book I. 47: the square on the hypotenuse is equal to the sum of the squares on the other two sides) or arrived at Thales' discovery that the diameter of a circle subtends a right angle at any point of its circumference. Again, the Babylonians, who had observed the movements of heavenly bodies for centuries and kept records of their observations, knew that solar eclipses recur after each period of 223 lunations. Thales' successful prediction of a solar eclipse (probably that of May 28, 585 B.C.) may have been based on his knowledge of the cycle established by the priestly star-gazers of Babylon. But the latter, so far as we know, never dreamed of making such a use of their huge accumulation of facts about the apparent movements of sun, moon, and stars as (1) to arrive at the conclusion that the sun, not the earth, was the central body, (2) and to attempt a calculation of the comparative dimensions of sun, earth and moon. Any such efforts to explain the observed facts would have seemed as impious to them, no doubt, as it did to the ecclesiastical opponents of Galileo.

It is impossible to give in this chapter even the simplest outline of the history of Greek mathematics during the period, between three and four hundred years, of what can only be called radio-active thought, so swift and brilliant and penetrating did the Greek spirit prove itself in this domain of imaginative intelligence. All that can be done is to indicate the authors and dates of a few outstanding achievements. By the middle of the fifth century before Christ Hippias of Elis, Hippocrates of Chios, and Democritus had investigated two famous problems in geometry; (1) the trisection of any angle, and (2) the duplication of the cube. Plato, the famous philosopher (427–347 B.C.), was not himself a mathematical discoverer, but he had a great enthusiasm for mathematics, and encouraged his pupils to specialise in some branch. To the aspiring young astronomer he set the problem of ascertaining the real, uniform, and orderly movements which would account for the apparent motions of the planets. We come next to Eudoxus (408–355 B.C.), one of the greatest mathematicians of all time and, among the Greeks, the equal in power and originality of the immortal Archimedes. He made two great and far-reaching discoveries, which not only insured a further rapid advance in Greek geometry, but also entitled him to be regarded as a pioneer of ultra-modern mathematics. His theory of proportion, applicable to incommensurable as well as commensurable magnitudes, is still accepted as bed-rock work after the lapse of twenty-three centuries. And his method of exhaustion for measuring curvilinear areas and solids, to which Greek geometry was so largely indebted, brings the mathematician within sight of the infinitesimal calculus of Newton and Descartes. Is it not amazing to know that there was a thinker living in the fourth century before Christ who could have understood and appreciated Newton's "Principia"?

In astronomy Heraclitus of Pontus (388–315 B.C.), a pupil of Plato, made a notable advance when he discovered that the earth rotates on its axis once in twenty-four hours and that Mercury and Venus are satellites of the sun. Menæchmas, a pupil of Eudoxus, discovered the conic sections a little later. Then came Euclid (he flourished about 300 B.C.) whose masterpiece is too well-known to require praise or description. Excepting the Bible, no book has lasted so long and influenced so many minds, and it is still doubtful whether Einstein's theory of space will in the end displace Euclid's. Between Euclid and Archimedes comes Aristarchus, who insisted that the sun, not the earth, is the centre of the planetary universe, the latter revolving about the former like the other planets. He also calculated the sizes and distances of the sun and moon, and here his results would have been correct if certain angles in his hypothesis (*e. g.* the angle subtended by the diameter of the sun or moon at the earth's centre) had been accurately determined. The saying that history repeats itself is curiously illustrated by the experiences of Aristarchus and Galileo, separated though they be by so vast a gulf of time. Aristarchus might have anticipated the famous *E pur se muove* of Galileo, if the Stoic philosopher Cleanthes, who thought he ought to be condemned for impiety on the score of setting in motion the immovable "Hearth of the Universe" (the earth, of course), had had the spiritual authority and temporal power of the Church of Rome in the sixteenth century.

Archimedes is the last of the Greek master-mathematicians and the greatest of all. The stories about him show how profoundly his contemporaries were impressed by his faith in the power of science and his absolute devotion to the quest of truth for truth's sake. "Give me a place to stand on and I will move the earth," he said, having in his mind the principle of the lever. This anecdote gains in point when we remember that his contemporary, Eratosthenes of Cyrene, had, by noting the difference between the shadows cast by the sun at Syene and Alexandria, estimated the diameter of the earth at about 7,850 miles (only 50 miles less than the modern measurement for the true polar diameter). Archimedes was killed at the sack of Syracuse (212 B.C.) and the story of his intentness on a diagram in the dust after the capture and his brusque order to the Roman soldier to "stand away" from it is quite in character. His tubular screw for pumping water (which is still used) and the engines, equivalents of our modern artillery, which he invented during the siege, thus for a long time foiling the attacks of the army of Marcellus, show that, as in the case of Kelvin and other great modern mathematicians, there was a keen practical side to his genius. He was a master of both pure and applied mathematics. He founded the whole science of hydrostatics, and wrote the first treatise on mechanics. But his greatest achievement perhaps was the development of the method of exhaustion invented by Eudoxus which enabled him to ascertain accurately the surface and volume of a sphere, the areas of segments of a parabola, and a spiral. When translated into the terms of modern analysis, his solutions amount to actual operations in the Integral Calculus! His heart was in pure science rather than in its practical applications to war or industry, and his choice of an emblem to be engraved on his tomb—a cylinder circumscribing a sphere, with the ratio which the volume of the former bears to the latter's—aptly illustrates his spiritual outlook. He could foresee, no doubt, that it was the creation of new methods of truth-seeking, not the results of immediate practical value, which counted for most at the long last in the service of mankind. I can imagine him smiling at the truth latent in the fabulous toast of certain Cambridge thinkers: "Here's to pure mathematics, and may they never be of the slightest practical value to anybody."

After Archimedes the only outstanding name is that of Apollonius of Perga, called the "Great Geometer," who gave us the complete treatise on conic sections, inventing the explanatory names of parabola, hyperbola, and ellipse. Then Greek mathematics gradually ceases to be progressive for various reasons. The work already done was filled out in detail, new curves were invented and measured, and the beginnings of Algebra were introduced. But the lack of a better notation (such as came later on in the Arabic numerals with the wonder-working zero) and of the systematic use of symbols was a real obstacle to further advance. The Arabic scientists, working on a basis of Greek culture, were to carry the torch of mathematical discovery onwards and upwards in the centuries to come. But there is no more surprising victory of the Greek spirit of truth-seeking for truth's sake than the mathematical activity which, in less than 350 years, rose from the land-surveying of the Egyptians and the sterile star-gazing of the Babylonians to brilliant anticipations of the achievements of Copernicus and Galileo, Descartes and Newton.

II

The Greeks from the first had a singular power for accurately depicting animal forms, which was manifestly the outcome of a careful observation of the living types. Perhaps they derived this faculty from the Minoan race whose culture they inherited. The vases of the sixth and seventh centuries before Christ show us wild beasts in action, every feature of which, even to the dentition and the texture of fur or skin, is portrayed faithfully. Here, then, was the observant eye at work in a way not to be equalled from the art of the other peoples in the civilisation of the Mediterranean. Some of the earlier treatises in the Hippocratic collection (of which more anon) contain a rough classification of living creatures, especially fish, which shows that the science of biology, as we understand it, was already in becoming, if not in being. Our wide use of the term " biology " would not, however, have commended itself to the ancient Greek. With them the word " bios " connoted the life of man only; and, furthermore, they were only interested in the lives of other animals in so far as they ministered to the welfare of what was to them the central and all-engrossing figure in the universe, " man the measure of all things." Just as the Israelites discovered God, so the Greeks discovered Man—and the latter discovery, when we remember how our " miserable bodies " have been despised and debased by Oriental peoples and under the Christian dispensation, might well rank as the most important of biological triumphs.

The scientific biologist arrived at the height of his power in the person of Aristotle, the greatest mind of antiquity—perhaps of all the ages that have been. Aristotle was no physicist, and the necessity of clearing the ground from his monumental misconceptions in that domain caused his biological work to be long ignored or underrated. The modern estimate of his achievement as biologist is set forth in a letter written by Darwin to Ogle in 1882: " From quotations I had seen I had a high notion of Aristotle's methods, but I had not the remotest notion what a wonderful man he was. Linnæus and Cuvier have been my two gods, though in very different ways, but they were mere schoolboys to old Aristotle." Next to Darwin's epoch-making works, Aristotle's is now the most widely-read of biological treatises. He was not immune, needless to say, from the picturesque and popular errors and legends of his age. Goats that breathe through their ears, the salamander that walks through fire, the stag caught by music, the vulture impregnated by the wind, the unicorn, the mantichore—these denizens from the far-Eastern or Egyptian wonderlands, far beyond his horizon of inquiry, appear in his great History of Animals. Again, to take a deeper view, the way in which his philosophy dominated his science may have postponed for many centuries the coming of that tremendously effective "working hypothesis," the Theory of Evolution. The trend of all Aristotle's thought was teleological; he saw the universe moving to an end in itself; "it moves like a thing beloved," he says, in an access of the Platonic inspiration which never quite left him. There was no room in his vast and ordered system for a theory of the survival of the fittest. There could be nothing unfitted for its ultimate purpose in the cosmos as he saw it in his mind's eye. Empedocles, thinking that we have no right to believe, for example, that rain falls to make the crops grow in spring any more than it does to spoil the stooks in autumn, had a very different view of the world about him. And he at any rate anticipated the Darwinian hypothesis—that the fit and the unfit are produced together, that the former survives and the latter perishes.

But the merits of Aristotle's natural history far surpass its incidental faults. It is impossible here to give an adequate appreciation of a work which, because of its minute observation and many scraps of homely wisdom (some of them ancient saws), often recalls the charming dissertations of the great French naturalist, Henri Fabre. It may well be that the happy study, to take one particular point, of Mediterranean sea-life, the curious results of which are here revealed, took place during his long honeymoon with his fair young princess by the much-murmuring sea in the Isle of Mytilene. That may have been the happiest period of his life—a joyous open-air holiday from which he gathered sun-born energy for the great tasks to come, the teaching of Alexander the Great, and the instruction of the Hellenic and Hellenised cities from the Lyceum. He would hear what the fishermen had to say, and then look into things for himself (which was Fabre's method). His story of the fishes is a prodigious array of curious facts, carefully collected and collated, and it is surprising how often what appeared to be some small inaccuracy turns out to be a scrap of the truth which had to be re-discovered in modern times—for example, it is quite clear that he knew by sight the little transparent creature which becomes an "elver" or tiny eel, the discovery and identification of which are one of the lesser triumphs of modern research. Again, he is well acquainted with the strange metamorphoses of insects, and there are many Fabre-like touches in his life-history of the gnat, which must be throughout the outcome of his own pertinacious observation. And of the cicada, whose dry sharp chirrup was unpleasing to Browning's ear but doubtless music to Aristophanes (see his "Birds"), he gives a complete and accurate account, noting how it was absent from treeless lands, such as Cyrene, and never heard in deep sunless forests, but at its best in olive-groves, for the foliage there is sparse and the sun comes through. In bringing together all this lore of natural history—a subject a little contemned, perhaps, by the Greeks, who had not the Roman liking for country life—Aristotle sets biology by the side of the august science of astronomy and bids us look for beauty in the little things near at hand. "The heavens," he says, "are lofty and remote, and of heavenly things the knowledge that our senses give is sparse and vague. The living creatures, on the other hand, are at our very door; and if we so wish, we may have ample and accurate knowledge of them all. We take pleasure in the beauty of a statue; then shall not the living fill us with delight? and all the more if in the spirit of philosophy we search for causes and recognise the evidences of design."

III

In medicine, again, Greek practice was based not on theory, or what can only be called religious magic (as in the Middle Ages), but on the accumulated results of careful observation. Only they among the peoples of antiquity had, not "medicine-men" in our anthropological sense of the term, but "physicians" (the word is derived from *physis* = Nature) who regarded diseases as natural phenomena (not as punishments for sin or the results of supernatural possession) to be cured or alleviated by means suggested through nature-study. Hippocrates, who was a great traveller, being called in, no doubt, to cure patients of high position in the various city-States, and died in extreme old age at Larissa about 377 B.C., was a veritable brother in art and science of our own great Sydenham, the founder of the modern clinic. Indeed, he was the Father of Medicine in the modern sense of the scientific term, and he was one of the greatest men that ever lived. He had many disciples, who followed his method faithfully, and the Hippocratic corpus, a collection of about seventy different works, contains the gist of their massed experience and the results of the "inductive" method of investigation which was consistently and continuously pursued by the Hippocratic school.

The spirit of the work of Hippocrates and his disciples, perhaps the noblest manifestation of the Greek conception of man's duty to man, is expressed in the "Hippocratic Oath":—

"I swear by Apollo the healer, and by Asclepius, and Hygieia, and Panacea, and all the other gods and goddesses . . . that, according to my ability and judgment, I will keep this Oath and this agreement —to count him who taught me this art as dear to me as my parents . . . to look upon his offspring as my own brothers, and to teach them this art, if they would learn it, without fee or stipulation. . . . I will follow that system of treatment which, according to my ability and judgment, I consider for the benefit of my patients, and abstain from whatever is injurious and mischievous. I will give no deadly medicine to any one if asked, nor suggest any such counsel; nor will I aid a woman to produce abortion. . . . Into whatever house I enter, I will go there for the benefit of the sick, and will abstain from every act of mischief and corruption; and above all from seduction. Whatever in my professional practice—or even not in connection with it—I see or hear in the lives of men which ought not to be spoken of abroad, I will not divulge."

It is the Magna Charta of Medicine, and in every age and country it has been religiously kept for the benefit of practitioners and patients alike. If Hippocrates had done nothing more in his long and laborious life-time than formulate this ideal of the good physician's duty to suffering humanity, he would yet be among our greatest benefactors.

The Hippocratic practice, moreover, was so sagacious and scientific that modern medicine has been defined as a return to it! Hippocrates and his disciples lacked, of course, many of the modern practitioner's advantages. The reverence felt for the dead, which is so deeply rooted in the Greek mentality, prevented the dissection of human bodies, though not of an animal's. Yet the descriptions of cases in the Hippocratic collection are essentially modern in their patient, disinterested observation of symptoms and in their capacity for seizing on the essential fact. The descriptions of diptheria and typhoid are absolutely accurate. There can be little doubt that a patient taken to one of the Asclepian temples (really the Greek equivalents of our hospitals, but better furnished with fresh air as a rule) had a far better chance of being cured than any eighteenth-century sufferer. Except that he employed bleeding too freely (though never to the extent customary among us a hundred years ago) there was little fault to be found with the Hippocratic physician's remedies and palliatives, for he fully recognised that he was, after all, only Nature's assistant.

Galen (A.D. 130–202) had neither the scientific intelligence nor the moral greatness of Hippocrates, but both the earlier and the later exponent of Greek medicine would have deplored the mediæval use of their treatises which substituted for minute observation the authority of the written word and its traditional interpretation.

In modern times philosophy has been a study for specialists with a terminology which baffles the man in the street and the man at the club window. Now and again a professed philosopher has influenced the lives of his pupils who learnt to "envisage" things from his point of view, to talk or write in his language, and to believe that their master had "cornered the Absolute" and guessed the ultimate secret of the universe. T. H. Green of Oxford and M. Henri Bergson are examples of the teachers of philosophy whose influence extended far beyond the four walls of their class-room. The former must have been the last in that succession of remarkable men, beginning with Wycliffe and including Newman, who were accepted at Oxford as repositories of the living truth, whereby men may better their lives and rebuild the world nearer to the heart's desire, to that vision of the fair, far City of God which has always haunted mankind. In point of fact these famous teachers won their hold, in the first place, by the force and fascination of character—by the "beauty of holiness" in one or other of its bright manifestations—rather than by their peculiar and personal views on the world within and the world without. To be like them, not to believe as they did, was the essential thing. Despite the appearance of such teachers, however, philosophy has been in modern times a pursuit detached from the great issues and interests of everyday life. But there are signs of a change in the general philosophic outlook to-day—for the dominating schools of philosophy are more and more inclined to admit that the vital test of any principle is in its helpfulness in the art of living and to state their conclusions, as far as possible, in the language of ordinary people. That is to say, we are returning to the point of view of the ancient Greeks to whom philosophy was the " love of wisdom " that its name implies —the earnest and enamoured quest for the truth which enables men to live in harmony with the unseen powers about them and with one another. Hence the vital importance, for the present age of spiritual unrest, of a study of the Greek philosophers.

It was about 600 B.C. that the first attempts were made by Greek thinkers, looking at things as they are, to construct a theory or working hypothesis of the universe. To the Greeks the curiosity to know the causes of phenomena and to probe their inner nature came as inevitably as it does to a small boy of to-day who breaks up a toy engine to see how it works. "It was wonder," writes Aristotle, "that first led men to philosophy." It is not necessary to enter into a discussion of the speculations of the philosophers of Miletus, the capital of Ionian commerce and colonial enterprise, where the great merchant-princes provided them with a cultured audience and the means of support. It is important, however, to note that the edifices of thought they built up were very different from the imposing cosmogonies of the Eastern world with which, until the conquests of Alexander the Great, the younger West had no contact. In the East philosophical systems were created by priestly guilds, whose profound intent it was to provide the spirit of man with a retreat, a peaceful refuge, from the toils and distractions of life. In the Greek West, on the contrary, the earliest philosophies were the work of single souls, free and unrestrained by religious sanctions in the use of reasoning, and the saying of one philosopher, "Man is the measure of all things," was tacitly accepted by all, since philosophy was regarded as the master-science of living. The Eastern cosmogonies are piled heavenward, like the Himalayas, and we see them white with the snow of eternal thought, remote from the bustle of everyday life and inaccessible save to the spiritual acrobat who turns his back on his kind. But the Greek philosophies are road-side temples

—impressive in their marmoreal beauty, no doubt, but open to every wayfarer who wishes to step inside, and open to the sunshine and the quick air.

It was the rise of the "Sophists," however, which gave the great impetus to philosophical thought at Athens and elsewhere in the fifth century B.C. The name they go by had not the evil significance it possesses to-day, for they provided a society without universities or printed books with what is now called higher education. Since every citizen took a speaking part in politics and had to plead in person in the law courts, oratory was a necessary accomplishment, and instruction in the art of persuasive speaking was the basis of the course provided by a sophist for his pupils. Gradually these teachers fell into disrepute for three reasons—first, because many of them taught how an audience might be deceived by rhetorical cleverness; secondly, because they sold their wisdom for money, often making very large sums; thirdly, because they lacked as a rule any kind of local patriotism. Plato gives us an interesting portrait of Hippias, one of the most famous and prosperous of the Sophists. He was a master of every kind of knowledge known to his world, and he was an excellent speaker and lecturer as well as a many-sided craftsman. Even in his old age he had such a powerful memory that, after once hearing a list of fifty names, he could repeat them accurately in the order in which he heard them. On one occasion, when he went to the Olympic games (the Greek world's fair—not merely an athletic festival) all he had on his person had been made by himself. No wonder that this master of all arts and crafts (including that of making lots of money) found well-born, well-to-do pupils whereever he went, and received the honorary citizenship of many cities, both great and small.

Socrates, who was deeply interested in all arts and crafts and in teaching his fellow-mortals, was the greatest of the Sophists. But he did not take money from his pupils and was not content with the showy, superficial knowledge which makes for immediate political success. So he escaped the condemnation of Plato who gave the word "sophist" the bad meaning which it has kept ever since.

Socrates, as we see him through the eyes of his disciples, Plato and Xenophon, is one of the most impressive figures in the world's history. Like Buddha or Mahomet, both of whom he exceeds in intellectual stature, he was able to change the trend of civilisation by his personality as much as by his doctrine. Xenophon shows him as deeply interested in such practical matters as housekeeping and military tactics. Plato, on the other hand, presents him as pre-occupied with the problems of knowledge, morality, and politics,

He was a valiant soldier, a very Odysseus for endurance and a person whom no enemy cared to meddle with—we see him in the retreat from Delium, where the Athenian army was badly beaten, "stalking like a pelican and rolling his eyes," as if he was merely walking through the Athenian streets, and making it very clear to the pursuers that he could, and would, make a very stout resistance if attacked. Again, we see him at the siege of Potidæa standing fixed in thought from one sunrise to the next and thinking out some profound problem—in one of those strange ecstasies, no doubt, which are recorded in so many stories of mediæval saints. But Socrates was no ascetic, for we also meet him at a dinner-party, where he goes on drinking and arguing till day dawns and the other revellers drop off to sleep, all except Aristodemus who gets up and follows him, as his habit was. Alcibiades, the most brilliant of all his disciples, thus describes his person and his charm of personality: "I say he is exactly like the busts of Silenus, which are set up in the statuaries' shops, holding pipes and flutes in their mouths; and they are made to open in the middle, and have images of gods inside them. I say also that he is like Marsyas the satyr. You will not yourself deny, Socrates, that your face is like that of a satyr. Yes, and there is a resemblance in other respects also. Are you a flute-player? Yes, you are, and a far greater virtuoso than Marsyas. He, to be sure, used to charm the souls of men with his compelling breath in his instrument and the players of his music do so still. But you produce the same effect with your words only, and do not require the flute: that is the difference between you and him."

Socrates was not like a modern philosopher who works in a study and sets forth his views in books. He spent his time discussing anything and everything, in the market-place, in the gymnasia, and other places of public resort. His mission was to convince the world of its ignorance (or its half-knowledge, which may be a more dangerous thing) by the conversation method (dialectic), by asking and answering questions, treating the most absurd or outrageous opinions with tolerant respect, and with unruffled patience exposing the fallacies underlying them. He compelled his opponents in a disputation to try to define their terms, never resting content until his principles "stood firm, not only for the moment but for evermore." If the eternal truth proved to be elusive, he yet demonstrated, by practice and by precept, that the quest for it was man's first and last duty. To love wisdom and pursue it all one's life, even if the absolute truth turned out to be unattainable, was the most profitable lot—just as the love of a perfect woman, even if she is never won, may yet be the most liberal of educations for a young man. Socrates also believed, and taught others to believe, that character as well as intellect is necessary to philosophic achievement. He lived for truth, and when he was condemned for corrupting the minds of young men (a judicial crime, no doubt, but the times were critical and the authorities anxious and perplexed) he met death with a valiant and serene mind. In his last hours of life he discussed the problem of immortality, but—as a final proof of his passion for the truth—would not allow himself to be over-persuaded by comfortable thoughts, as is constantly the case with old men who die to-day. The story of his end, told by his disciple Phædo, is perhaps the greatest passage in secular literature.

It is to Plato, one of the aristocratic followers of Socrates, that we owe most of what we know about this martyr to truth-seeking. Plato travelled for twelve years after the death of his master, and on his return to Athens bought a house and garden in a public park called the Academy, and lived there for the rest of his life, studying and lecturing on all the branches of knowledge, especially astronomy and mathematics. His school in the Academy was a sort of university without fees; it survived, in some form or other, for nearly eight centuries.

Plato, in whose twenty-seven dialogues Socrates is always the protagonist, is really a philosophic poet with an incomparable gift of style. "The truth and splendour of his imagery," said Shelley, "are the most intense that it is possible to conceive." For him, as for his master, philosophy is always a "way of life." From Socrates he had also learnt that goodness is knowledge, and that the only secure foundation of conduct is a comprehension of the principle of good in itself as well as in its applications. Therefore he sought the knowledge which would reveal the ultimate truth of the universe as ideal goodness and be the objective, the inspiration and the aspiration, of all human endeavour, the individual's and the city's alike. Where, then, was this knowledge to be found in the fluctuations of opinion, in the perpetual ebb-and-flow of circumstance? In attempting to answer this question he was led to the belief in a world which contains, as everlasting realities, Forms or Ideas, of which the qualities we recognise when we call an action *good* or a picture *beautiful* are changing and imperfect copies. And these eternal originals the soul of man knew before it was born into the flesh, and it must return to a knowledge of them, through the shadows or copies which make up the universe perceived by the senses, by the power of reasoning. It is a theory which has influenced poets and preachers, more than any other, to this very day, and it is one of man's inevitable moods. St. Paul was expressing the self-same doctrine when he wrote: "We look not at the things which are seen but at the things which are not seen; for the things which are seen are temporal; but the things which are not seen are eternal." Plato's philosophy or poetry, call it which we will, is part of the very texture of Christianity as a way of life. In the wonderful parable in which Plato describes the adventures of the soul before birth and shows how beauty recalls the world of ultimate truth (Good at the core of all being) he sets forth for all time the grounds of the faith of the Idealist who turns from the visible to the invisible, from the ephemeral world in which we live to the eternal heaven in which we cannot die. He was careful to show how his theory helped men to be virtuous, and for that reason he faces (as every Greek did) the problems of politics. His ideal State, where philosophers are kings, ceases to seem fantastical when we remember that the Greek philosophers always submitted their theories to the ultimate test of living them. Some of his thoughts are of vital consequence to-day—for example, his diagnosis of the unsatisfactory nature of commerce and industry as due to the root-fallacy of treating them as money-making affairs, not as a means of benefiting the whole community.

If Plato was the first great Idealist, Aristotle was the first Realist! Aristotle always has a foot on earth, Plato uses his wings fearlessly. I have already discussed Aristotle's contribution to mankind's scientific knowledge, and all his philosophic inquiries start from a basis of observed facts—the facts that were momentary and illusive matters to Plato, mere copies of realities. Aristotle's works, again, have nothing of the literary charm of Plato's; in point of fact, some of them are merely dry lecture-notes. His best books are his "Ethics" (edited by his son Nicomachus), "Politics," "Poetics" and "Rhetoric," which still have an imperishable value as text-books. The first is an admirable introduction to the systematic study of morals; the second, though narrowed to the range of the Greek city-State, is the best prelude extant to the study of political science; the third and fourth are monuments of literary criticism which can never be surpassed. He never ignores mundane matters, yet is no materialist; seeing as he does man's highest happiness in the activity of the loftiest part of his nature—*i. e.* reason, which, in Aristotle's sense, is almost equivalent to our "spirit." And he says:

"Such a life is higher than human. For a man will live it in virtue of something divine in him and not of his humanity. If Reason compared with our human nature is divine, then the life of Reason is divine in comparison with human life. We should not listen to those who tell us that human beings should think like men, and mortals like mortals, but we should achieve such immortality as we may, and strain every nerve to live by the highest things in us. They may be small in substance, but in price and power they are far beyond all else."

Both Plato and Aristotle, who are really complements of one another, were men in touch with the "great world" of their times. Each had a chance of training the ideal ruler. When sixty years old Plato was asked to undertake the education of the young prince of Syracuse, but the attempt was a failure. But Aristotle was the tutor of Alexander the Great, whose very crimes, so nobly repented of, add to his nobility. In him the wealth of Greek moral and intellectual culture was grafted on the passionate heroism of Achilles, his favourite hero, and Aristotle had good cause to be proud of a pupil whose moral character was a marvel to his own and all the pre-Christian ages. This achievement alone would have justified the philosopher of the Lyceum.

Both to Plato and to Aristotle philosophy was a "way of life," but in each case the teacher's appeal was rather to those who wished to live the life of a thinker, out of the dust and uproar, than to men of action. Moreover the old city-State was disappearing in the clash of the larger polities, which was destined to be swallowed up by all-conquering Rome. A spiritual city of refuge came to be sought from the blood-and-irony of life, and Greek philosophy—never divorced from the busy world of men—hastened to provide a choice of havens, the Heaven of the Christian being as yet unthinkable. In the generation following that of Aristotle and Alexander the Stoic and Epicurean systems attempted to satisfy the ethical need. Both systems had a lasting influence, reaching far into the Christian era. To the Epicurean (unjustly contemned in the modern use of his name, especially when worn down into "epicure") true wisdom consisted in the rational enjoyment of all life's good things—not the mere gratification of the senses, but the rewards of passionless self-esteem, such as study and social intercourse. Stoicism, however, which attracted the Roman temperament, was by far the more influential. It appealed to the will, which was a man's very own, unconquerable by the pangs of tyranny or the pains of disease. Once more the old opposition was revived: Epicurus was the Realist; Zeno of the "Painted Porch" at Athens, where he taught for half a century, was the Idealist. And the Greek thinkers, or the thinkers in Greek, who succeeded these two, kept to the end the characteristics of the Greek philosopher—passion for truth at all costs, and the feeling that no wisdom was worth while which could not walk in the ways of men.

In recent times the plays of the great Greek dramatists—Æschylus (525–456 B.C.), Sophocles (496–406 B.C.), Euripides (480–406 B.C.), and Aristophanes (446–385 B.C.)—have been reproduced in such a way as to give students a new insight into the significance of these famous masterpieces. The Cambridge University revivals have been especially interesting, thanks to the natural capacity of the young actors shown even in the female parts, the scholarly efforts to make the costumes and scenery archæologically correct, and the excellent music by famous composers such as Sir Hubert Parry. At Cambridge these ancient plays are given in the original Greek, but the provision of line-by-line translations, the Greek and English on opposite pages, has enabled packed audiences to follow the tragical or comical argument. The revival of the comic—almost farcical—"Birds" of Aristophanes, which first took place in pre-war days and was repeated in 1923, amused even those spectators who could not follow the verbal wit and humour of the dramatist. Extraordinary costumes had been devised, and the bird chorus with their fantastical head-dresses and wings, showing all the hues of the rainbow and several others, surprised everybody present with an amazing series of kaleidoscopic colour-schemes. A well-known dramatic critic, who is quite Greekless, confessed that he was as much entertained by this " Gilbertian fantasy " as by Rostand's famous bird-play.

Even more remarkable was the elaborate Cambridge production of the " Oresteia "—the sequence of three tragedies by Æschylus in which King Agamemnon on his return from the taking of Troy is murdered by his wife, Clytemnestra, and avenged by his son; Orestes is then pursued by the Furies for the sin (to modern ideas unpardonable) of killing his mother and is in the end released from their pursuit by the interposition of Apollo. The scene in front of the Palace at Mycenæ, when Clytemnestra welcomes Agamemnon and Cassandra, his share of the Trojan captives and his paramour, into the house of death was tremendously impressive. The young men who played the parts of Clytemnestra and Cassandra, which lie almost beyond the scope of a modern actress's art, were successful beyond all expectation.

Professor Gilbert Murray's verse translations of the plays of Euripides have provided Miss Sybil Thorndike and others with opportunities of showing their capacity of interpreting these ancient masterpieces under modern theatrical conditions. But the nearest approximation to Greek methods of production is to be seen at Bradfield College where, once in every three years, a Greek play is presented. A theatre has been made there in an old chalk-pit, which is an exact model of one of the open-air theatres that still exist in a more or less ruined state in Greece and in the lands formerly called Magna Græcia. As you sit and watch the play (the "Antigone" of Sophocles was the last one produced by the Bradfield boys) from one of the grey semi-circular stone benches under quicken boughs, through which the sunlight filters down and bird-song mingles with the stately music, you can believe that you have crossed the gulf of more than twenty centuries and are a Greek at home in some Greek city. But only for a moment—for even a Bradfield production is an artistic compromise between ancient methods of dress and acting and the usages of the modern stage. Then in the famous chalk-pit everything is on a smaller scale both in space and time. At Athens perhaps fifteen or twenty thousand spectators would assemble in the early morning and sit there till dusk, for it was customary to produce the work of three selected poets, and each of them presented four plays, a trilogy of tragedies and a "satyric" piece as a conclusion, in which the action was comic and the chorus consisted of satyrs or half-wild "salvage men," followers of Silenus and boon lieges of the great God Pan. Nevertheless these modern productions, even when presented in a modern theatre and with the use of an English translation, will enable the student to realise the nature of Greek drama better than any written exposition. If you wish to understand how near to us in some respects, and how remote in others, these ancient masterpieces are, you must seize the opportunity of seeing a Greek play actually performed. And whatever you feel about it, you will at any rate admit that Greek drama, within its limitations, was dramatic to a degree!

In ancient Greece there were only three actors (excluding the members of the chorus) on the stage at one time, never more. They wore buskins (*i. e.* wooden soles about six inches high) and padded their chests to look more imposing. They also donned strange linen masks, with wide mouths and emphasised features and portentous cone-shaped projections above, very like the horns of a mediæval lady's head-dress. Their movements were slow and stately. There was no acting in our sense of the term, nothing of what is called "business" by modern players. Emotions were depicted by changes in the voice, to which the Greeks were far more sensitive than we are. The scenery was extremely simple. Beyond the front circle of marble seats, where sat the notable people, was a circular space (the "orchestra") in the midst of which was the altar of Dionysus (Bacchus), god of wine and of the spring-tide blossoming. Beyond this space was a long narrow stage in front of a wooden building, on the wall of which a temple or a palace was painted. If characters inside the house who were dead had to be shown, they were brought out on a kind of low trolley.

The actors were supplemented by a chorus of fifteen persons. These danced or went through intricate movements in the orchestra, and sang choral songs when there was a break in the action, if you call it action; their leader was the mouthpiece through which they sometimes conversed with the chief characters. The speeches were longer than those in a modern play; they were uttered, no doubt, with an elaborate elocution. Often the dialogue was conducted in alternate lines, a sort of verbal thrust-and-parry. The catastrophe was never shown on the stage; it was generally described by the Messenger, a stock character, whose long speech was an invariable convention. The music, in which smaller intervals were used than those to which the modern ear is accustomed, would probably strike us as very unpleasant could we hear an example of it. The Greek tragedies, if you compare the number of lines, were much shorter than "Lear" or "The Duchess of Malfi." But the slow and stately movements of the actors and their elaborate elocution, which could not be eked out with gesture and was the result of years of careful training, caused the former to be played more slowly. The absence of women's voices and other allurements, for the female parts were played by males, and the complete lack of subsidiary plots or comic relief cause the Greek masterpieces to lack the rich variety of Shakespearean plays. But they gained in intensity by the absence of all forms of distraction, except the moralisings of the chorus, and they must have tortured the attention of an audience able to comprehend all the subtle vicissitudes of emotion and thought, mood and method, which the best of modern scholars perhaps merely apprehends. These ancient tragedies can still come to life and deeply stir our emotions, as the modern revivals show beyond a shadow of doubt. And the success of the French classical dramatists, even if it be only a *succès d'estime* to-day, makes for the conclusion that the barest form of Greek tragedy still possesses a deep vitality and may some day be used, amplified and amended, for the expression of new dramatic purposes.

Thirty-three of these plays by Æschylus, Sophocles, and Euripides have survived. This is only a very minute portion of the whole number presented, for every March twelve new plays were enacted in the great theatre of Dionysus at Athens, and they continued to be written even in the Christian era. Some of the best examples may have been lost; for two of the finest extant —"Œdipus the King" by Sophocles and the "Medea" by Euripides—did not win the first prize in the annual spring-tide competition.

The subjects of Greek tragedy were taken from the legends and legendary history which were a common possession of the Greek race. Fiction was tabooed, and the "Persian Women" by Æschylus, which was inspired by the Greek victories in 480 B.C. over the Persians, is the only tragedy extant the subject of which was taken from the history of the author's own times. The English Oratorio, which takes its subject from the Bible or from Biblical history, provides a parallel not only to this restricted choice of themes, but also to the conventional form in which they were treated. The matter of the Greek tragedies puzzles a modern reader by its primitive elements mingled with thoughts and subtleties of emotion which are at times more profound than anything to be found in our Elizabethan dramatists. The gods and goddesses of Olympus appear, and they have not much progressed in morality since the time, centuries before the Athenian prime, of the Homeric poems. None the less, there are passages of moral reflection and exhortation which give the lie to these fair, strange Presences who only differ if at all from mortals in their omnipotence and power of foreseeing the future. After all, the Anglican Church service, which rehearses psalms that are appeals to a fierce tribal deity and is at the same time inspired by the Sermon on the Mount, may vex students in distant centuries with the same sense of incongruity. In the fifth century before Christ the whole intellectual atmosphere of Athens was transformed, thanks to the vast self-confidence engendered by the victories over Persia, to the stimulus of Ionian culture, and to that contact with other cities and peoples which was the result of the rapidly-expanding interests of the Athenian Empire. Athens became the capital of Mediterranean civilisation, the clearing-house of religious and moral ideas, whatever their source. Spiritual evolution was speeded-up into a sort of revolution, the like of which has never been seen in any other age, and the gulf between the outlook of Æschylus on things human and divine and that of Euripides is almost as wide and deep as that between, say, Shakespeare and Shaw. Criticism, in its most intensive form, caused the primitive superstitions to melt like snow in warm sunshine, though some of them still remained in the high places of an Athenian poet's mind like snow-drifts in the shadow of moorland rocks. We see the many Greek deities becoming the aspects of one God and that God ceasing to be mere superhuman power moved by human motives—lust, love of praise, revenge—and becoming a power that makes for righteousness, using his incalculable power in wondrous ways to reward justice and punish injustice. The primitive things in Greek tragedy can be overlooked, since the woof and warp of what happens in them is the stuff of that human nature which has changed so little (if, indeed, at all) in three thousand years. These plays are always a criticism of life in some soul-searching crisis. There is nothing theatrical in the problems proposed for solution, and they are solved in accordance with the laws of human nature—not with any of the absurd trickery, having no relation whatsoever with real life, which is the curse of the modern stage. Just as there was no scope in the acting for what we call "business" (the Greek opinion of all such brisk stupidity would have been much the same as Duse's), so the "clever curtain" is unthinkable in Greek tragedy. The three great Greek tragedians certainly fulfil Matthew Arnold's definition of the permanent quality in all literatures. "The poet," says that famous critic, "has in the first place to select an excellent action; and what actions are the most excellent? Those, certainly, which most powerfully appeal to the great primary human affections; to those elementary feelings which subsist permanently in the race, and which are independent of time. Those feelings are permanent and the same;

that which interests them is permanent and the same also. . . . To the elementary part of our nature, to our passions, that which is great and passionate is eternally interesting; and interesting solely in proportion to its greatness and passion." The thirty-three tragedies we inherit from ancient Athens might be defined, collectively, as social history—in the same sense that Hardy's novels are the social history of Wessex—lifted to the plane of the loftiest poetry. The spiritual progress they illustrate is shown in three stages by the three masters.

Æschylus was middle-aged when he fought at Salamis and Marathon. He thought much more of his war experiences than of his dramatic successes (the first in 484 B.C.) and his epitaph records only the fact that he fought against the Persians. His drama is rudimentary, for his characters are little more than incarnations of their ruling passion, and the choral lyrics, which are more majestical and momentous than those of Sophocles and Euripides, are a great part of each play. Three vital conceptions—*Ate*, the law of blood for blood; *Hubris*, the insolence that breeds sin and brings punishment; and *Sophrosyne* or the golden mean which is the root of all virtue—run through the whole of Greek tragedy, but the first two are most prominent in the Æschylean dramas. Æschylus also accepts the primitive idea of a curse pursuing a family generation after generation, provoking its members to rush with blind infatuation into the courses that lead to ruin. We still cherish this notion in a different form, either quoting the scriptural text, "The fathers have eaten sour grapes, and the children's teeth are set on edge," or appealing to the Law of Heredity. Do we not believe that the Stuarts, the Bourbons, the Hapsburgs, and other famous families were infected with a family taint of folly, or worse, which brought about ever-recurring disaster? *Hubris*, the insolent self-sufficiency which is bred of great prosperity, is also an idea which survives in modern thought, and the conviction of Æschylus that excesses arising out of the overweening confidence in one's star (such as Napoleon's) engendered sin is likewise shared by modern thinkers. Even the idea of *Ate*, or blood revenge, which was being mercilessly criticised by Euripides only a few years after the appearance of the "Agamemnon," Æschylus' greatest tragedy, is not altogether extinct in these days when the Christian virtues are the basis of private and public morality, even where the Christian faith is no longer a vital, all-pervading influence. Wars of revenge (*revanche*) are not unknown, and the old doctrine of blood revenge can be traced, howsoever adroitly camouflaged, in the arguments in favour of the legal death penalty. Again, in the struggles between "Reds" and "Whites" in Continental countries, it has re-appeared in all its primitive ruthlessness.

It is from the idea of the necessity of blood for blood that Æschylus draws some of his most tremendous effects. He was unerring, despite his crude stagecraft, in the treatment of a dramatic situation; as Euripides said of him, he always did the right thing, without knowing why. Grant his premisses and the storm of emotion he depicts follows in accordance with the stern logic of circumstance. Clytemnestra slays her husband, and their son has the choice between slaying the murderess or being haunted by his father's ghost. Yet he knows that, if he kills his mother, he will be pursued by the Furies, the horrible incarnations of remorse which haunt the matricide. The "Libation-bearers," in which his spiritual struggle is depicted, is uncanny and terrible beyond anything in Elizabethan drama. The king's ghost is restless, crying for blood, and sending his wife ill dreams; Orestes and his sister are seen at the grave, communing with the restless spirit; Clytemnestra pleads with her son for her life and is driven into the palace to die, where her paramour, Ægisthus, perishes with a dreadful sigh; and as the dead bodies are shown before the palace door, Orestes is seen:

> "Streaked with his mother's blood, but striving hard
> To tell his story ere his reason goes."

In the third play the deities interpose and Apollo

purchases peace for Orestes from the Furies by giving them an established position in the hierarchy of immortals, as it were. In the "Prometheus," however, the "unconquerable mind" of man is vindicated, and the hero defies the tyranny of Zeus, who has inflicted on him an everlasting torture, almost in the spirit of the great chorus in Swinburne's "Atalanta in Calydon" (a finer example of the imitation of a Greek tragedy than Milton's "Samson Agonistes" or Hardy's "Tragedy of the Queen of Cornwall") which concludes :—

> "We all are against Thee, against Thee, O God most high!"

Here, amidst the incredible details of a strange Greek legend, a modern idea emerges triumphantly.

Æschylus is the most dauntless of the world's poets, ancient or modern. He is as familiar with Gods and Furies and Titans "whistling murder" as with men and women. His style is as stupendous as his argument; his metaphors have an epic grandeur which no other poet, not even Homer, attains so often as he does. In boding words he shows us the giant shades of Fate, piling doom on doom, and the anguish of his characters is repeated in agonies of the inanimate. Every other line is mighty in the sense that we speak of Marlowe's mighty line.

Little wonder that Browning found this colossus of language more impressive than Dante or any of the Elizabethans and confessed :—

> " Æschylus' bronze-throat eagle-bark at blood
> Has somehow spoilt my taste for twitterings."

To turn from Æschylus to Sophocles is like waking on a sunny morning after a stormy night vexed by nightmares. Sophocles was a popular citizen who held high office at Athens, proving himself the kind of official any good Athenian would make. He won the first prize in the first competition he entered, and to the very end of his long life was singularly successful in pleasing the judges. Two of his best plays, the " Philoctetes " and the " Œdipus at Colonus," were written long after his eightieth year. Devout in his orthodoxy, he never perplexed his audience with Æschylean speculations or with the unexpected questionings of Euripides. He was one of the " happy poets " ; for, though he saw evil rife in the world, he would not allow his sweet reasonableness to be embittered. *Sophrosyne*, the sagacity of " nothing too much," is for him the beginning and end of such virtue and welfare as men may achieve, and Matthew Arnold praised his mellow wisdom as it deserves :—

> " Be his
> My special thanks, whose even-balanced soul
> Business could not make dull nor passion wild ;
> Who saw life steadily and saw it whole ;
> The mellow glory of the Attic stage,
> Singer of sweet Colonus and its child."

He does not trouble the soul with "shadows of a magnitude" as Æschylus does, nor does he set us questioning all accepted beliefs, as does Euripides. He is the most commonplace man of genius who ever became a consummate master of his art. In the first place, he is a poet with a technique always sufficient to itself—mystical when he chooses, or delicately musical like an Æolian harp in a rose-scented breeze. He can feel, but he cannot think; there is no high philosophy at the back of his poetry.

To be able to feel and to make feeling a noble contagion, however, is the dramatist's greatest gift. No amount of thinking by itself will enable a writer to make a drama to stir men's hearts. Sophocles has a great gift of characterisation; his characters are living, breathing men and women in whom, no doubt, the Athenian spectator noticed a likeness to his own friends and enemies. And within the limits of the legend he has taken for his plot, Sophocles allows his people to say and do what they choose. He was also a master of stagecraft. His "Œdipus the King" is one of the best-constructed plays which have ever been written. The steps by which Œdipus is shown to be the slayer of his own father and the husband of his own mother in "Œdipus the King" are very complicated—yet the spectator of the play can follow it all, without feeling that the "long arm of coincidence" is at work.

When Orestes returns to avenge his father, pretending that he is a stranger bringing home the ashes of himself killed in a chariot race after great athletic triumphs (so as to deceive the guilty mother, Clytemnestra) the difficult problem presents itself of bringing about his recognition by his valiant sister, Electra. He had intended to hide his identity until vengeance had been accomplished. It would have been very bad art to have made him declare himself or be recognised by somebody else. Sophocles finds the most natural and affecting solution. When Orestes puts the urn supposed to contain her brother's ashes into Electra's hands, she is so overcome by sorrow that he cannot hide his own feelings, and so the recognition—a stock convention in Greek drama—is unconventionally effected. It is a lesson to the modern playwrights who so often prefer technical ingenuity to the simple, natural solution. His great dramatic invention was the Sophoclean irony, which is an ambiguity of language, or action, or situation. Œdipus curses the unknown murderer of his father, King Laius, and lo! the murderer is himself. Ægisthus, who has married Clytemnestra and knows Orestes to be his enemy, prepares to gloat over the latter's corpse, and the ground of his apparently safe sovereignty gives way under his feet, for it is really his queen's bleeding body. Of course, the quick-witted audience was in each secret; for Sophocles knew well, better than most modern playwrights, that you must never keep your audience in the dark.

Euripides was a student, a pupil of Socrates and one of the "intellectuals" of his day, and he was an infrequent prize-winner in the great spring-tide competition. He was a Futurist in fact and unpopular, and did not come into his own until the next generation. He was acted, or at any rate read, when his great predecessors were neglected as valuable antiques, praised, but not borne in mind. He alone of the Greek tragedians can appeal to the "giant heart of memories and tears," which is the consciousness of modern humanity. Yet his recognition to-day, after so many centuries, is due to the stirring poetical translations of Professor Gilbert Murray rather than to his own liberalism of outlook. He is comparable with Mr. Bernard Shaw in that he submits the orthodoxies of his age to an acid criticism, and so often gives us a discussion instead of action. He is comparable with Ibsen in that he brings the heroism applauded by the low-grade intelligence of the mob into the uncompromising light of day. The legendary personages are rationalised, as it were, in his plays: Agamemnon becomes a ruthless egoist, Menelaus a poltroon, Odysseus a master of *real-politik.* He takes war as it is—not the diversion of heroes intoxicated with the joy of battle, but a horrible savagery which looses all evil passions, ruins conqueror and conquered alike, and brings innocent women and children into a squalid slavery. His "Trojan Women," in which Astyanax, the little son of Hector and Andromache, is ruthlessly murdered (for Odysseus says that, if he lives, the Greeks may have the Trojan war over again), is the deadliest indictment of war ever known. Again, his plays are full of studies of oppressed women; some of them—Medea, for example—become fiend-like under the strain. He brings homely folk into his plays and also children, thereby preparing the stage to admit to its liberties all the possible and impossible types of humanity. He is not a master of stagecraft—chiefly because, in order to placate his audience, he had to introduce conventional endings, which are out of keeping with what precedes them. Criticism, after all, is not a merit in a dramatist who, if he wishes to be acted at all, must use the stuff of the age in which he lives as the substance of his drama. In the Euripidean drama, moreover, the chorus merely provides charming interludes of song and dance, which have little connection with the plot. As a poet, finally, he is not in the same rank as Æschylus or even Sophocles. Aristotle, the first of literary critics and perhaps the greatest of all, said of him: "If a bad manager in all other points, Euripides is at least the most tragic of all the poets." Indeed, he forgets the rule of "nothing too much" in his habit of accentuating pathos until the pain for a sensitive reader becomes intolerable.

Aristophanes, the greatest comedian ancient Greece ever produced, was an enemy of the "intellectuals" of his period. He would have said, had he been living to-day, that the plays of Euripides were actionable as well as actable. It is a question which he disliked most—Socrates or Euripides, both of whom he holds up to the ridicule of plain, honest folk. At the great feast of Dionysus in April comedies were performed, and eleven of those written by Aristophanes have come down to us. The work of his predecessors, unfortunately, and of the rivals who often beat him in the annual competition survives only in fragments. His comedy is the broadest buffoonery—often indecent baboonery—and the point of many of his jests has been lost in the long efflux of time. It is easy, however, to appreciate the rollicking speed and spontaneous gusto of his farcical plays, and also the cleverness of his Gilbertian plots. His predecessors are forgotten, and he had no successor. He stands alone in Greek literature, as Gilbert—like him an artist in verse-making—seems likely to stand in the history of the English stage. His best work was accomplished under the dark clouded sky of the Peloponnesian war, and the "Peace" and the "Acharnians" are Stop-the-

War plays. Extremely interesting, and at times ultra-modern, are the three plays in which women predominate; in the first putting an end to the war, in the second having their parliament, and in the third attempting to punish Euripides for traducing their sex. Euripides passed for an anti-feminist. Aristophanes, in addition to his other merits, was a great lyrical poet; that is why Heine compared him to a grove of singing nightingales and chattering apes.

But the modern theatre owes nothing to this solitary genius, unless we choose to consider Gilbert as an unconscious disciple. It is from the "new comedy" of Menander (343–291 B.C.), which took its subjects and characters from every-day life, that the modern comedy of manners is ultimately derived. His plays were once utterly lost, but large fragments of them have recently been recovered from the dust-heaps of Oxyrhynchus in Egypt. The author of the epigram, "Whom the Gods love die young," he had a style of "beautiful translucency" (Meredith's phrase) and was the Molière of his times.

Chapter VII — Greek Art

All Greek art at its best is a revelation of the Greek spirit with its characteristics as I have defined them. The measure and balance, which are in statuary the exact equivalent of *sophrosyne* in the sphere of conduct, of the works of the great century of Greek sculpture that have survived (for the most part in copies) never degenerate into convention. The masterpieces are alive; the untiring Caryatid of the Erectheum actually seems to breathe, drawing her breath easily, under her huge, eternal burden. There are other points to be remembered in these too few surviving masterpieces, whether they be statues or painted vases or temples or coins. Thus they always have the quality of serviceableness, that is to say, each after its fashion is subordinated to the greatest art of all, the art of living. The idea of a picture intended to sit on an easel, not to be used as a decoration, not to be lived with, would have seemed absurd to the Greek mind. So also would the modern custom of immuring works of art in a crowded museum. Again, all distractions from the simple, dominant motive were rigorously avoided. An anecdote of a great Greek painter illustrates this characteristic. He had painted the figure of a Satyr, beside which, as a trifling proof of his virtuosity, he had placed a partridge. But when he found the life-like quality of the partridge distracted attention from the Satyr, he painted it out. Thirdly, the beauty of the naked human figure—so familiar to the Greeks as never to be a provocation to unclean thoughts—dominated Greek sculpture and painting. As a matter of fact, the Greek body was itself a work of art, the greatest of all; its rounded muscles and elastic outlines are the deliberate product of centuries of open-air exercises in the creative sunshine. No wonder, then, that the sight of the tangible masterpieces of Greek art have always awakened an intense wonderment in those who see them for the first time. Renan, remembering in tranquillity the group of temples at Athens and the emotions they inspired, wrote:—"The Western world seemed barbaric, the Orient shocked me by its ostentatious pomp and its impostures, while the majesty of the best Roman seemed only a pose compared with the ease and simple nobility of the citizen who could comprehend what made the beauty of the Parthenon."[1] And even in these days of intense individualism in art, the Greek masterpieces remain an inspiration to all artists, even to a Rodin or an Epstein.

[1] "The Poetry of Architecture," by Mr. Frank Rutter in the People's Library series contains an admirable chapter on Greek architecture.

It is impossible, however, without abundant illustrations to enter into the vast and intricate subject of Greek statuary, vase-painting, etc. But Greek poetry is a master-key to all the splendour and significance of all Greek art; the more so because the Greek language was the most plastic medium of the kind that has ever been evolved from the consciousness of a race. Let me, then, supplement the brief study of the Greek dramatists by an account of the achievements of four poets, each unique in his or her mastery of the most universal of the arts.

Homer is the greatest of all the epic poets, and he has left us the earliest pictures of European civilisation. Both as poetry and as history the "Iliad" and the "Odyssey" hold a place apart in world-literature, and it is appalling to think what would have been the consequences if they had not been preserved.

To the Greeks Homer was *the* poet, just as to us the Bible is *the* book; and they, like us, have often found a deeper significance or a more poignant consolation than was originally intended in plain words which have gathered, in the long succession of time, a charm of association and the added beauty that is memorial. Moreover, these truly great poems, temples open to sunshine and sea-breezes, and built of noble numbers, have been models for the epic in every western age that knew them or the works that perpetuated their pattern (*e. g.* Virgil's " Æneid "). It is probable that we should never have had the " artificial epics," as they have been called, of Virgil, Lucan, Dante, Milton, and the rest, if the Homeric poems had been lost. It is even possible that such a loss would have prevented the " grand style " of poetry from being consciously cultivated. But what perhaps illustrates the enormous influence exerted by those happily preserved masterpieces of man's imagination is this strange fact—that even in the workaday world of to-day plain people know the meaning of the adjective " Homeric," though they may not have read a single line of any translation of Homer. We all know what is meant when a speaker or a writer alludes to " Homeric grandeur " or " Homeric laughter," or observes that " Even Homer sometimes nods." Furthermore, the chief Homeric characters are known to us all for their predominant qualities; Achilles for his valour, Helen for her beauty, Ulysses for his resourcefulness, Penelope for her faithfulness. Any orator, even if his pedestal be only a soap-box at a street corner, can use one of these names to point a moral; they are as familiar on our lips as the names of Hamlet or Pecksniff, Othello or Micawber. There are no better stories to be found in books; no personages better worth knowing. In Achilles we have a hero indeed; lacking the Christian gentleness that is an aureole about Lancelot's bowed head, it is true, but though barbaric in the violence of his anger and his unrestrained sorrow, yet a glorious fighter, a gentleman unafraid of the early doom ordained for him (even his chestnut steed knows all about it), capable of the tenderest compassion and of high-born courtesy to a suppliant enemy. In Ulysses, again we meet the heroic adventurer, bravely enduring all the toils and terrors of a world that is still half wonderland; a lover of his wife, too, to the end, and unable to find, even in the embraces of an ageless goddess in her garden-close in a fairy isle, any cure for his homesickness—for, if he had no word equivalent to our "home" on his lips, yet he had the thing itself in his much-enduring heart.

Then there are the Homeric women, fair and wise and holy—hardly equalled for noble simplicity in the long galleries of heroic womanhood from Sophocles to Shakespeare. There is Andromache, the loving young wife and mother who, in losing her chivalrous and valiant Hector, loses all that makes life worth living. There is Penelope, lacking nothing of the gentle dignity of the lady of a great house, even when that house is invaded by turbulent suitors who waste its substance and seduce her serving women, utterly destroying the kindly discipline of the household; keeping under hard trial her beauty and her honour, the respectful affection of her son, Telemachus, and her loyalty to her long-absent lord.

Then there is the maiden Nausicaa on the eve of a fair marriage—perfect in her sense of household duties, her virginal delicacy, her charming common sense, her gracious and generous courage. Above all and before all there is Helen, the innocent cause of the wars of the Greeks and Trojans, who is all the more impressive because we see so little of her, and because Homer, unlike the makers of mediæval romances, is far too wise to attempt a catalogue of her charms—here is an early example of the "nothing too much" which is the secret of so many triumphs of Greek art! Because of this reticence the beauty of Helen has lived through the ages and made flaming altars of the hearts of innumerable poets.

Sappho, though only three of her Odes—the third not long ago discovered in the Egyptian sands—have come down to us complete from the seventh century B.C. with a number of fragments, is none the less *the* poetess to us as she was to the Greeks. This wonderful singer—

> "Sappho, with that auriole
> Of ebon hair on calméd brows,"

(as her English sister-amorist saw her in a poetic vision) is one of the tragical heroines of world-romance; she died for the love that is the burden of her incomparable lyrics. "Her speech is mixed with fire," said one ancient critic. Here is a night scene of hers translated by Sir Edwin Arnold:—

"The stars about the lovely moon
Fall back and vanish very soon,
When round and full her silver face
Swims into sight, and lights all space."

And here, translated by J. H. Merivale, is a fragment from an Epithalamium, a form of poetry invented by the Greeks to glorify the at-one-ment of man and woman:—

"Sweet Rose of May, sweet Rose of May,
Whither, ah, whither fleet away?
What's gone no time can e'er restore—
I come no more, I come no more."

The melody of the original, like amber beads falling in a silver basin, and the intensity of the emotion behind it all, are but faintly suggested in these versions. One of her Odes, however, has been finely rendered as follows:—

"As the Gods thrice happy the man appeareth,
Who thy voice like heavenly music heareth;
Sitting near thee, surely no more he feareth
Sadness or anguish.

"Ah! thy laugh delectable, how it trances!
I am silent, scarce can I bear thy glances;
Wild my fond heart beats to behold thy glances;
Madly I languish.

"Parched and numb, the tongue to my palate clingeth;
Straightway subtle flame thro' my body springeth;
In my ears a tremulous echo ringeth,
Night cometh o'er me!

"Blinded, shaken, nought any more discerning,
Pale as moor-grass, seared by a mighty burning,
At Death's door, and strange to myself with yearning,
What may restore me?"

The sweet terror of the presence of the Beloved

has never been more poignantly presented, except perhaps by Apollonius of Rhodes in the passage which describes the awakening of virginal love in the heart of Medea at the first sight of Jason—"Who ever loved, that loved not at first sight?" as our Marlowe says! In the first stanza of the newly discovered ode are images that recall those in the Song of Solomon:—

"I have compared thee, O my love, to a company of horses in Pharaoh's chariots."

"Who is she that looketh forth as the morning, fair as the moon, clear as the sun, and terrible as an army with banners?"

Sharon was land-locked, but Lesbos in the sea; so that *the* poetess who has thus added to the world's slender store of universal love-poetry, seeing the white wings coming and going on the blue waters, compared *her* darling with a fleet of ships also.

As a master of the choral ode, lyric poetry in its loftiest form, Pindar (521–441 B.C.) is unrivalled in the world's literature. Four books of his odes survive, corresponding to the four great athletic festivals at Olympus, Delphi (Pythian games), Nemea, and the Isthmus of Corinth—festivals at which the spectator forgot that he was an Athenian or a Spartan or a Theban, remembering only that he was a Greek among Greeks. Pindar's poems are all in honour of some athletic victory and they were written to order, the poet himself travelling all over the Greek world to supervise in person the performance of them when the crowned victor entered his jubilant native city (through a gap in the wall made to admit him) or was entertained at a great banquet by his fellow-citizens. They were sung—and danced—while, to quote one of the Olympic Odes, "the beautiful beams of the fair-visaged moon lit up the dusk, and the whole city rang with joyous feasting." The existence of these wonderful poems serves to remind us that what is called the "athletic craze" to-day was also a feature of Greek life, and that the successful athlete was even more highly honoured among the Greeks than he is among modern Englishmen. People go to-day in their thousands and tens of thousands to see the revived Olympic Games (another legacy from ancient Greece) or a big boxing contest or a Final Cup-tie. But our greater poets do not regard these affairs as fitting themes for their finest poems, though Mr. John Masefield has written a small epic of "chasing," and Mr. J. C. Squire has celebrated the Oxford and Cambridge "Rugger" match in most exhilarating verse, and the late Rupert Brooke once promised to go with the writer to watch a championship boxing contest and make a poem about it—a promise that could never, alas! be fulfilled owing to the outbreak of the world-war and the poet's lamentable death in the Ægean. It is true that Euripides and other critics of established institutions and practices deplored the popularity of athletes on the score that they were "reasonless animals," did no useful work, and could not bear the hardships of a campaign as well as the ordinary citizen who had never been put through a course of artificial training. Still the average Greek who loved to watch the young men exercising in the palæstra, rejoicing in the sight of the "human form divine" unveiled and in action, would probably have blamed our poets and painters and sculptors for their comparative indifference to the artistic side of athletics.

Pindar, as the late Andrew Lang would insist, was no sportsman, though he made his living out of sport; at any rate he tells us nothing about the technique of boxing, wrestling, running, chariot-driving, etc., as practised in ancient Greece. It is highly probable that they did not know as much as we do about the science of athletic arts—for example, there is a Greek vase which shows us the finish of a sprinting race, and all the competitors are making their final effort for a win on the post in a way which Alec Nelson, the famous Cambridge coach, or any other trainer of modern Olympic champions, would think hopelessly bad form. Also there is an epigram in the Palatine Anthology which tells us how a would-be winner of an Olympic crown entered for the long-distance race, with five others, and came in seventh—for his trainer ran with him all the way and, though he was wearing a great coat, was ahead of him at the finish. Such modern refinements as the choice of a second or a third string, to act as pace-maker in the mile or the three miles, were quite unknown to the Greeks. I have a strong suspicion that a team of Olympic victors from ancient Greece, could they be brought across the Styx to the Wembley Stadium, would be hopelessly out of it with the least distinguished representatives of modern athletes—except, perhaps, in the all-in fighting (pancration), in which a competitor could do anything, even to using his teeth, to overcome his opponent. But however that may be, the cult of athletics is a tradition derived from Greek antiquity.

Pindar is the most difficult of Greek authors, and there are no English translations which give a just impression of his magnificent but involved and highly allusive manner of writing. He is more concerned with the athlete's family tree and the legendary history of his city than with the athletic achievement which was so honourably rewarded. He was an aristocrat of the aristocrats, the scion of a priestly family, and there was a certain justice in the comment of a young Eton scholar on his Odes—"old Pindar might have written them to be sung in a church, I mean a temple." He is constantly moved by a passion of patriotism, and the loftiest thoughts of this "electric Pindar," as Mrs. Browning called him wisely and well, are like dazzling flashes of lightning out of a blue sky. His Odes have strangely impressed modern poetry—thus he was consciously imitated by Dryden and Gray, though neither they nor any other modern writers have ever succeeded in exactly copying the complex forms, architecture in a sense, of their Greek master, nor have these latter-day imitators glorified, as Pindar did, the physical excellences which seemed virtues of the body, yet true virtues for all that, to the ancient Greeks, who never forgot that there is nothing to be ashamed of in our human flesh.

A much later Greek poet, who was the originator of a mode of poetry that still survives and flourishes, is Theocritus (born about 305 B.C.) whose Idylls in the Doric dialect are indeed a joy for ever. In his days the ancient Greek cities had lost their independence, and Alexandria rather than Athens had become the metropolis of Greek literature. Greece was no longer a political force, but a world-conquering culture which enlisted literary recruits everywhere. Alexandria was a veritable factory of books, under the patronage of the Ptolemies, and in its atmosphere of *belles lettres* every conceivable form of literature was produced in profusion. Theocritus, who came from Sicily and must have been primarily inspired by Sicilian folk-song (which survives to this day as a poetical motive-power), was a favourite at the Syracusan and Egyptian courts. The twenty-nine poems attributed to him include not only pastoral pieces, but also "mimes"—*i. e.* poems which illustrate the manners and customs of the time and its every-day joys and sorrows in a dramatic fashion. Simætha and her maid Thestylis using magic to recover the love of Delphis and bring him back to her, the very aspect of that night of jealousy and hope commingled is brought before us in Simætha's farewell to the moon:—

"Lady, farewell: turn seaward now thy steeds.
As I have purposed, so shall I fulfil.
Farewell, thou bright-faced moon. Ye stars, farewell,
That wait upon the car of noiseless night."

Thus, in a few words, after the manner of the Greek poets in all ages, he produces as strong an impression of a night of moonlight perplexed with mortal love as Shakespeare does by the long dialogue between Lorenzo and Jessica in "The Merchant of Venice" which begins:—

"The moon shines bright. In such a night as this,
When the sweet wind did gently kiss the trees,
And they did make no noise—in such a night
Troilus methinks mounted the Trojan walls,
And sigh'd his soul toward the Grecian tents,
Where Cressid lay that night."

Mighty is reticence, and the Greeks are the masters of it to the end of time! As alluring as his pastorals are the mimes of Theocritus, of which the poem describing the visit of Gorgo and

Praxinœ, two Syracusan women staying at Alexandria, to the palace of King Ptolemy to see the newly and gloriously robed statue of Adonis, is an entrancing *genre* picture, and as modern as any of Anstey's "Voces Populi." The chatter of the two women in the house from whence they start through the crowded street to the thronged palace is eternally true to nature, for two Scots ladies visiting the wonders of Wembley would discourse on the self-same topics, the stupidity of husbands and the laziness of servants and so on. Annoyed by their clack, a stranger exclaims: "You wretched women, do stop your incessant chatter. Like turtle doves you go on for ever. They are enough to kill one with their broad lingo—nothing but *a, a, a*." The Doric of Theocritus is to the Athenian mother-tongue very much what the Scottish language is to classic English, and its broad melodious words, dropping like honey from the honeycomb, are a fascinating feature of the pastoral poem. The long list of the sons-in-art of Theocritus includes Virgil ("Eclogues"), Milton ("Lycidas") and Matthew Arnold ("The Scholar Gipsy").

For a vivid insight into Greek life, however, we must study the four thousand epigrams of the Palatine Anthology, which cover a period of ten centuries. They are not epigrams in the modern sense; they do not carry a sting in the tail. Again, brevity is the soul of their beauty; they are not bundles of rhetorical lines; they have the simple dignity of a Greek coin; created by a single impact, or so it seems, they have the ring of a token of pure gold. Some of them have been imitated by poets of all times and all climes, but the original always remains unrivalled. The epitaphs have all the peculiar virtues of Greek art. Few indeed are the English verse memorials which make sorrow concise yet all-conquering as they do—perhaps Browne's tribute to the Dowager Countess of Pembroke and Landor's to Rose Aylmer come nearest in form to the best Greek models, though the hyperbole of the former and the egotistical melancholy of the latter would have been repugnant to the Greek spirit. Here is a typical example of Greek brevity and aloofness :—

> " These piled-up stones the boy Cleœtes hide;
> Pity him, who was beautiful and died."

It is well-nigh impossible to English the epitaphs adequately. Shelley's version of one of Plato's two famous epigrams :—

> " Thou wert the morning-star among the living,
> Ere thy fair light had fled;
> Now having died thou art as Hesperus, giving
> New splendour to the dead."

and William Cory's rendering of the tiny threnody by Callimachus which begins :—

> " They told me, Heraclitus, they told me you were dead;
> They brought me bitter news to hear and bitter tears to shed.

I wept as I remembered how often you and I
Have tired the sun with talking and sent him down
the sky,"

are poems in themselves and, even though the simplicity of the originals has been lost, must count as victories. After all, as a famous Greek scholar once said, you cannot translate a star into a flower. The love epigrams are not quite so difficult—the danger there arises from the difference between modern love of women, which is an intellectual thing, and the simple sensuous emotion of the Greeks to whom woman was merely a unique chattel. Ben Jonson lifts this emotion to a higher plane, when he adapts Philostratus in "Drink to me only with thine eyes," but otherwise goes the right way to work. Plato's other epigram of the enraptured lover, who cannot see enough of the beauty of the Beloved, has been admirably Englished as follows :—

"Thou gazest on the stars :
Would I might be,
O star of mine, the skies,
With myriad eyes,
To gaze on thee."

Of two epigrams which touch on the loves that must be bought I myself have made these versions :—

(1) "Danæ in her golden tower,
Married an immortal shower.
If you would your love enfold
Be, like Zeus, a shower of gold."

(2) "Love inflicts a twofold curse—
A heart on fire, an empty purse.
Would I could from passion fly
And live at peace in poverty."

The Palatine Anthology provides an inexhaustible store of themes; many of the dedications, for example, which show us a soldier hanging up his bow and quiver in Apollo's temple or the faded beauty resigning her looking-glass to Aphrodite, reveal the Greek tradition with a finger of light. And there are humorous epigrams, most of them late ones, such as the following by Lucilius (first century A.D.) :—

"Some say, Nicylla, that you dye your hair:
Those jet-black locks you purchased at the fair"—

which have been imitated century after century, until in some slightly-changed form they reached the lips of the modern red-nosed comedian.

* * * * * *

It is impossible to follow the trend of Greek art, even in poetry and prose only, till it lost the last flickering of the Greek spirit at Constantinople. It made converts everywhere; just as Mr. Joseph Conrad, a Pole by birth, writes in English, so Jews like St. Paul and Romans like Marcus Aurelius wrote in Greek. Only for a brief period in a small country were the Greek gifts regarded with suspicion, and refused—by the Maccabees in Judæa.

THE Roman, a type that endured for ten centuries, had not the creative intelligence of the Greek. He was a great artisan, but no artist; his chief ability was adaptability. He had not those wings of the mind which take a poet or a philosopher into the high, solitary places of contemplation whence this busy every-day world of ours is sent spinning " like a fretful midge "— wings which, even if they beat vainly in a vast inane, yet show man as a beautiful, if ineffectual angel. He had not the spiritual eye which sees and remembers some Platonic " idea " of ultimate beauty or the spiritual hand (for such it is) which patiently wrests a copy of it out of language or a palette or cold marble. Except in satire, supposing we do not derive it from the comedy of Aristophanes, he originated nothing new in literature. We have to look through his statuary, as Winckelmann did, in an age when the grandeur of Roman works of art seemed true artistic greatness, to find the forms of truth and beauty which were created in the brief Hellenic prime. There is more, perhaps, to be said for his achievement in architecture. The Greek temple was the final expression, complete in itself, of the Greek genius for architecture. But it had no future, it could not provide a line of development for the designing of great secular buildings, and there, it would seem, the Roman architects displayed a genius of serviceableness. The Romans, let us admit, were great builders as they were great road-makers and great engineers; their bridges, aqueducts, and wall-structures show it. Yet it is true, broadly speaking, that in the wide demesnes of art and science they were unimaginative and unprogressive and did little or nothing to carry on the work of the Greeks. Mr. Asquith, that ripe scholar who has tested the validity of his learning by using it in the art of living, thinks—it is not an original thought by any means—that Rome built the bridge over which many of the best thoughts and the finest models of antiquity found their way into the mediæval and thence into the modern world. Yet one has an uneasy feeling, even when disposed to grant this contention, that the Romans were dangerous, even destructive, intermediaries. The Hellenism they so eagerly adopted, even to the extent of identifying their indigenous deities with the bright and joyous denizens of the Greek Olympus, was never more than a thin veneering. The wholesale spoliation of Greece, the most shameless looting the world has ever seen, adorned the great houses of Rome with the masterpieces of Greek art, and had at any rate one effect that is good at first sight—the Roman plutocrats became interested in encouraging the production of Greek works of art. Yet a good case could be made out for the assertion that Roman patronage gave Greek art its death-blow. The Romans were not artists, nor even "amateurs" in the fine old sense of the term, and they despised the Greek sculptor or painter they patronised or the Greek philosopher they took into their opulent households as a teacher of youth or an intellectual valet (Lucian gives a sad picture of the wretchedness of such a dependent) as a "hungry little Greek" (*Græculus esuriens*). Next to the lust of power for power's sake, their contempt for the artist is perhaps the worst thing in Rome's legacy to the modern world.

As regards science the Roman mind was not creative and not to any great extent receptive. The idea of a cosmos, which could be understood by the use of reason, did not spring up naturally in Central Italy as it did in Greece. In medicine it is significant that the Romans, before the light of Greek culture broke into their darkness, were almost as backward as the African savages of to-day. Fever (*Febris*), That Tired Feeling (*Fessonia*), and even Bad Smell (*Mephitis*) were supplicated as deities, over whom the Goddess Safety (*Dea Salus*) presided in her temple on the Quirinal. *Lucina*, with a host of assistant goddesses, presided over child-birth. Cato the censor, who insisted that the ancient Rome he revered, guarding it from scientific innovations from abroad, could dispense with doctors and yet keep good health, gives some strange prescriptions. The cure-all for human patients, according to his ideas, was cabbage, and a dislocation could be reduced by reciting over it an incantation which sounds like a child's counting-out rhyme: *Huat banat huat ista pista sista domiabo damnaustra.* At a later period, however, when the Greek medical system had been to some extent adopted, the hospital was invented, the first motive being the wish to provide sick soldiers with treatment and so diminish the costly wastage of forces in the field or in garrison on the far-flung frontiers. These military *valetudinaria*, which were located at important strategic points, were excellently arranged and seem to have had drainage systems. Public hospitals on the same lines were established later on, and the mediæval "spitals" were imitations of them. No doubt the Asclepian temple of the Greeks was the origin of this hospital system, but credit must be given to the Romans for developing it on a large scale and, so far as we can see, on excellent hygienic lines. Generally speaking, however, even in the applications of Greek science the Romans were unenterprising, and there was no marked change for the better when Alexandria—the headquarters of science from the Hellenistic age onwards—was incorporated in the Roman Empire.

In the wide and wonderful demesnes of art and science, then, the Romans have given us very little—perhaps the Carthaginians, had they prevailed in the titanic contest for world dominion, would have been safer repositories of the Greek treasures of art, though in every other way less preferable as intermediaries. Yet the Romans achieved one priceless boon for the advancement of the world's civilisation. They realised in their private life an ideal of the family, as a nursery of kindly discipline and the simple, every-day virtues, which was far nobler than the best in the life of ancient Greece.

It may almost be said that the Romans invented home-life—the only possible work-shop for the making of the character that is destiny. The family was the unit with which the ancient Roman commonwealth was built up and from which it acquired its tremendous resistance-power against the assaults of enemies and the shocks of circumstance. The Roman *familia* was an ampler thing than the modern family; it included not only the parents and their offspring, but also all servants and dependants and the household deities as well. It was in the Roman's house (originally a kind of wigwam, perhaps) and in the countryside about it, not in a far-shining Olympus, that the kindly spirits of Latium (*numina*) dwelt and exercised a power that was as a rule beneficent. These deities were not created in the likeness of man, like the Greek gods and goddesses; they were impersonal spirits or influences, having will-power and haunting a spinney, a spring, a hearth, a doorway, a store-room. Religion to the Roman was the reverence for these various influences—a sense of the viewless bonds (*religio*—a binding-back) which were about him, like the silvery gossamer-threads floating in the still air of a bright far-listening morn. And the house itself was a veritable temple of these spirits—*Janus*, spirit of the door; *Vesta*, spirit of the hearth; the *Penates*, spirits of the store-room; the *Lares*, perhaps spirits of dead-and-gone ancestors; and the *Genius* of the father of the family, whose will-power enabled him to fulfil his duties and use his rightful authority aright. So the Roman house was a home indeed—a holy place, almost a holy of holies, and utterly unlike the home of a Greek citizen, who spent most of his time in the streets or market-place and merely used his dwelling as a place to eat and sleep in, as a repository for his goods and chattels and a work-shop for his wife and her hand-maidens.

Over all the human beings of his *familia* dwelling in this sacred hold the father had absolute authority, a power of life and death in practice as well as theory. In Cicero's time a senator put his son to death for taking part in Catiline's conspiracy, and it was held that he had not exceeded the legal limits of the *patria potestas*. The father could expose a child to die if he did not choose to be at the cost of bringing it up, and it was not until the Roman Empire became a Christian Commonwealth that this right was abolished. In theory this awful authority was too much to be entrusted to any human being; in practice, however, it was seldom or never abused. It was restrained by the traditions, to which it was the Roman habit to defer implicitly, and by the kindly influences of the household deities. It worked out as a kindly and ever-loving discipline which was an admirable training in all the public and private virtues that can be collectively described as patriotism. Roman children were not relegated to a nursery, much less packed off to a boarding-school before their 'teens. They were with their parents even at meal-times and allowed to listen to their talk. A good father, like the elder Cato, who said that a wife and a son are the holiest of all holy things, conducted his son's education himself, scorning to trust so sacred a privilege and responsibility to any slave. Rather than let his boy miss any of the heroic legends of the race, Cato wrote them all out in big letters with his own hand.

In early times marriage gave the power called *manus* to the husband, which meant that, in theory at any rate, the wife was also subject to the *patria potestas*. In practice, however, marriage was a real partnership—as in most Latin countries to-day, especially in France—and in accord with the inner significance of the famous phrase *Ubi tu Caius, ego Caia* ("Where you are the lord, I am the lady"). Divorce was easy, but most marriages were a success, and the familiar *S.V.Q.* (for *sine ulla querela*, "without a quarrel") on monuments erected by the surviving partner, husband or wife, must have expressed the truth much more often than not. The Roman husband may not have been demonstrative in his affection; the elder Cato had a saying: "Never kiss your wife except in a thunderstorm." But there can be no doubt whatever that the place of the wife and mother in the Roman household was much higher than in a Greek house, and was secured by long tradition and the influences of the home deities. Everybody had his or her place, and there was a place for everybody in the home thus constituted, and this bed-rock institution of Roman life well deserved the praise of Cicero, when he was pleading for the restoration of his house which had been pulled down by his political enemies: "Is there anything more sacred, anything more closely hedged round by every kind of sanctity than the home of each individual citizen? In that place he has his altars, his hearth, his household deities, his private worship, his rites and ceremonies. For all of us home is a sanctuary so sacred that to tear a man away from it is an outrage against the divine law."

Character was the chief product of the Roman home life; it was a nursery of the peculiarly Roman qualities, *gravitas, pietas, simplicitas, benevolentia. Gravitas* is not easily defined, though a glance at certain portrait-busts of Roman worthies tells us what it was. It was the feeling of responsibility in matters both great and small which prevents a man being carried away by ephemeral passions or the reckless enthusiasm which flouts old, well-tried traditions. Rome, like the essential Roman, was never in a hurry to make changes of any sort. *Pietas* was the habit of paying due respect to traditions and institutions and all duly-constituted authority. Æneas, Virgil's epitome of the race, was *pius* in the first place, not because he was a sanctimonious prig (as modern readers are apt to think, remembering his treatment of Dido), but because he was true to his faith in powers human and divine. *Simplicitas* was the quality of the man who will not be misled by any pompous look-see into losing his grasp of realities. It was a kind of heavenly homeliness. *Benevolentia* was the spirit of goodwill to relations, dependants and neighbours, the exercise of which made one happy in the happiness of others. The atmosphere of the Roman household fostered these homely virtues and made Roman character what it was.

Another quality of the Roman which differentiates him from the Greek was the love of the country and of country life. This also was an emanation of the life of the Roman father and his *familia* planted in the countryside and revering the spirits of meadow, woodland, and spring. The Greek was an incorrigible city-dweller; his estates were a source of revenue, not a pleasant retreat from the cares of business. But the Roman was intimate with Nature, could gather in the "harvest of a quiet eye," and find a wondrous refreshment for body and soul in the homely amenities of a country estate, if no larger than Horace's Sabine farm. The Greeks, it is true, admired the beauty and grandeur of Nature and wrote of it in immortal verse—but never with that loving intimacy which we find in the Roman poets. Nor was it only in poetry that the Roman's love of the country, so like the Englishman's, expressed itself beneficially. It made him profoundly interested in agriculture, whether he was a practical farmer like Cato, who loved the land, or a large investor in acres and the slave-labour with which to wrest profits from the soil. The Romans were the pioneers of organised agriculture, the first real experts on rural economy. Columella's treatise on agriculture, which is written in a style of dignified simplicity, can be read with profit even to-day. When the monasteries of St. Benedict's Rule, acting on the maxim that labour is prayer (*laborare est orare*), made grain-fields and orchards and vineyards out of swamps and wild wastes, they were greatly indebted to the practice and precept of the Romans.

Character was Rome's chief asset, the real "Fortune of the City," yet the days of her far-reaching greatness seem to present a picture of unbridled licence among the men and women in the world's eye. The city itself when Roman power was at its height was a maze of huge tenement blocks thronged by a proletariat living on doles of grain and kept amused by the brutal shows in the Colosseum and the orgies of immorality (perhaps non-morality is a juster expression) in the huge Baths of Caracalla. Rome is unique among the world's great capitals in that it has never become the seat of great industries. What are now called "luxury trades" were in the hands of the hordes of slaves in the great Roman houses, the owners of which, like Crassus, often made a large income by hiring out their skilled servitors. The Roman mob was necessarily idle and ill-contented, without employment or any chance of getting it. The plutocrat and the pauper met in the thronged thoroughfares, and their mutual hatred was inextinguishable. The women of fashion were heartless and abominably cruel, for such moral degeneration is the inevitable result of an unceasing close contact with a retinue of slaves. Comfort, except for the rich, was out of the question; even Martial, who was not poverty-stricken, had to be content with a third-floor flat. Home life was impossible on antique lines in the steep slums of the tenements—the Lares and Penates and the other gentle household spirits could not enter there. The block of flats is part, no doubt, of Rome's evil legacy to the modern world. Some of the provincial towns were also sinks of iniquity—Pompeii, whose intimate past has been exposed by the spade, was manifestly the home of a degraded populace. Yet, away from Rome and certain degenerate towns, the old tradition of Roman home life endured, and we should not be so often inclined to overlook that significant fact if the searchlights of the satirists and social historians had not been constantly directed to high-placed criminals, poisoners and adulterers and degenerate aristocrats or brutish plutocrats maddened with luxury, with the lootings of the whole world. The relations of the younger Pliny and his wife are an instance, however, of those which were invariable among the official classes in every stage of later Roman history. They were deeply in love with one another; when Calpurnia was away, he kept her portrait at his bed-side by night and would wander to her room by day through force of habit. Pliny, who was a type of the Roman permanent official, did not, we may be sure, follow the grim old Cato's advice to kiss one's wife only during a thunderstorm. Probably Cato himself did not live up to his aphorism.

Rome never produced characters of outstanding charm and noble persuasiveness; she provides no parallels to Pericles, Socrates, Epaminondas, Alexander the Great. Yet there are fine and impressive figures, some of them granitic in their greatness, in Livy's long portrait-gallery and in the vision of the makers of Rome which passes before the eyes of the dutiful Æneas in the Elysian fields :—

> " Quin Decios Drusosque procul, sævumque securi
> Aspice Torquatum, et referentem signa Camillum . . .
> Quis te, magne Cato, tacitum, aut te, Cosse, relinquat ?
> Quis Gracchi genus, aut geminos, duo fulmina belli,
> Scipiadas, cladem Libyæ, parvoque potentem
> Fabricium, vel te sulco, Serrane, serentem."

In Imperial times the Roman character is nobly exemplified even in some of the wearers of the perilous purple, and we have in Hadrian, that heaven-sent autocrat, a perfect type of the essential Roman, whose high qualities had a background of indefatigable *virtus*, the capacity to play the man at all times and in all places. He shared the hard life of his legionaries when in the field; he is said to have marched twenty thousand miles, on foot and with full military accoutrements. He was a mighty hunter. He wished to see with his own eyes all the wonders of the world—he ascended Mount Casius to see the sunrise and Mount Etna to see the sunset, visited the tombs of Pompey in Egypt and Epaminondas at Mantinea (that dubious stricken field!) and carved his name on Memnon's statue. He was passionately in love with all Greek art—as a boy they called him *Græculus*, the little Greek. He was interested in all religions, old and new, though a pagan at heart, and the tales in the Talmud of his talks with the Rabbis show how his tolerant curiosity impressed his contemporaries. In the person of Antinous he worshipped his ideal, neither Greek nor quite Roman, of the beauty of the human form divine. He died gallantly, after so many victories and experiences, jesting at the court physicians: "Too many doctors are death to an Emperor," and conferring a last boon, perhaps the greatest of all, on his country by designating the admirable Antoninus Pius as his successor. And he left us the plaintive, musical lines to his "poor little soul" which sum up the restless yearnings, in a tearful smile, ironical and anguished, of the pre-Christian Empire:—

> "Animula, vagula, blandula,
> Hospes comesque corporis;
> Quæ nunc abibis in loca?
> Pallidula, rigida, nudula,
> Nec ut soles dabis joca."

* * * * *

Roman law, which was Rome's one great and original contribution to the intellectual equipment of the world, grew out of the life of the Roman family with its traditions and strong sense of discipline. The father in his house was the first judge; and since, at any rate in the early stages of Roman development, none could challenge his power of life and death and the right to execute his judgments within the sphere of the *patria potestas*, he was an anticipation of the Imperial autocrats of the far future. The law that thus had its small, secretive beginnings was in a very real sense the crowning work of the family-engendered Roman character. It represented the accumulated results of Roman common-sense, itself a phase of Roman character, solving problems of man's relations with man as they arose and with infinite caution seeking a general rule from a mass of particular experiences. It was not the creation of great outstanding minds (Rome was sterile in the production of supermen as compared with Greece), but of the multitude of average citizens; that is to say, of the race itself. In the early days the State was just the family writ large, and disputes between citizens or offences against the commonwealth, which were from the first distinguished, were settled or punished in the spirit of the severe, but just, *paterfamilias*. Though all authority was concentrated in the father, to an extent unique in ancient societies, its exercise was limited at almost every point by ancestral custom. Thus, when a breach of discipline occurred within the family which had to be severely dealt with, a family council of all the grown-up male members had to be called and consulted by the father. If the wife's conduct was seriously in question, her male kinsfolk had to be summoned to consultation. The spirit of reverence for law in being and custom, which was so often law in becoming, created in the family an atmosphere of law-abidingness (if I may coin an ugly, but useful, term) which passed the portals of the home and was breathed throughout the city.

The Twelve Tables, compiled by the decemvirs in 451 B.C. and 450 B.C., were the earliest written law. Throughout Roman history this code was regarded as the foundation of the civil law (*jus civile*); that is, the law regulating the relations of Roman citizens (*cives*). When Cicero was a boy, he learnt its rhythmic sentences by heart; it was in many respects the equivalent as an instrument of education of our Catechism. On this rock, for the Twelve Tables were never abrogated, was founded the whole stately structure, a masterpiece of human intelligence and in its way a great work of art, which was built up without interruption through a thousand years until it reached its final form in the *Corpus Juris* of the Emperor Justinian (died A.D. 565).

Rome's earliest written code was the rigid and narrow affair which one would expect to find in a selection of recognised customs obtaining in a small and simple social organism. By the end of the Republican era not a single clause had its original meaning. Reverence for the letter was combined with a willingness to expand the spirit, when the case for any change had been demonstrated by experience, by means of the legal fiction, a device which has been freely used in English law. Adoption, without which a Roman family, continued only by male issue, might become extinct, was a notable instance of the legal fiction. So also was the acceptance, to take a later example, of the modifications introduced into the law by the answers (*responsa*) of jurisconsults which pretended to be strict interpretations of the traditional code.

Here a brief digression into the subject of the Roman constitution and the way it was adapted to new circumstances can be logically introduced. The Roman constitution, like Roman law, was not deliberately planned; Polybius points out that it was formed " not on a theory, but through frequent conflicts and actual crises," the sagacious course being chosen in each situation as it arose. The Roman, like the British, Constitution, was a tissue of illogical contrivances, antique survivals, and quaint political fictions. Even a Sulla or an Augustus was careful to introduce innovations of the most startling kind only under a show of constitutional precedent. The constitutional history of Rome, however, differs profoundly from that of Great Britain. "The great contests for freedom in this country," wrote Edmund Burke, "were from earliest times chiefly upon the question of taxing. Most of the contests in the ancient commonwealths turned primarily on the right of election of magistrates or on the balance of the several orders of the State." In the early stages of Roman history the struggle was to limit the *imperium* or authority [1] of the chief magistrate, for the centre of political gravity at Rome lay in the executive, whereas in England it lay in the legislature. The Roman *imperium*, howsoever and by whomsoever exercised, was in the nature of an autocracy, and the Middle Ages recognised this fact when using Cæsar (" Kaiser " or " Czar ") as the title of an absolute monarch and applying the name " Holy Roman Empire " to a State that was neither holy nor Roman nor even an Empire. The President of the United States is the nearest thing in modern constitutional theory and practice to the holder of the Roman *imperium*; if he and his authority were cut in two, each part would be a Roman Consul.[2]

Roman law, and its continuous evolution

[1] *Imperium* is " authority," *auctoritas* " influence."

[2] The dictatorship of Mussolini in Italy is an instinctive revival of the ancient form of Roman governance.

through the ages, is too complex and technical a subject to be dealt with at length in this primer. To the legal genius of the Romans we owe wills and contracts—the latter a really wonderful achievement; for, as Maine says in his "Ancient Law": "The positive duty resulting from one man's reliance on the word of another is among the slowest conquests of advancing civilisation." The whole trend of human history may be succinctly defined as a slow and often painful transition from status to contract; with set-backs from contract to status such as may be exemplified from the recent history of Trade Unions in this and other countries. In the epoch between the promulgation of the Twelve Tables and the fall of the Republic the most far-reaching legal development was that of the *jus gentium* or Law of Nations which arose out of the need for a law which should regulate the relations between resident foreigners, among themselves and with citizens, when Rome became a great commercial State (commerce was, of course, the real motive-power of its expansion, and it was in accordance with the Roman character to give the foreigner a square deal in disputes that might arise). The *jus civile* was reserved for citizens, but the *jus gentium* affected the former by degrees and eventually superseded it, because it came to be regarded as a universal code, based on principles of justice common to all mankind and so in harmony with the natural order of the cosmos. In the three centuries following the foundation of the Imperial system by Augustus, who granted official recognition to the jurists, the law was moulded into a logical system under the compulsion of unifying and interpretative ideas derived from Greek philosophy, especially Stoicism. Thus arose jurisprudence, that philosophy of law which seeks and finds the general principles of justice. Ulpian, one of the five great jurists—the others were Gaius, Paul, Papinian, and Modestinus, Papinian being accepted as the greatest of all—whose rulings were authoritative, was mainly responsible for incorporating the concept of a Law of Nature (*jus naturale* or *naturæ*) into the structure of Roman jurisprudence. This law, which embodied the universal rules of conduct, flowing from the nature of man as a rational creature, has profoundly affected political thought in Europe, and is even to this day a power in public morality. From the scientific view, no doubt, it is a gigantic fallacy, a beautiful but baseless mirage. Nature, as the scientist knows it, does not concede the "rights of man," and all we know of the history of primitive institutions contradicts the declaration (incorporated, for example, in the preamble to the written American Constitution) that all men are naturally born free. Yet it is by means of such strong fallacies that modern civilisation has reached its present plane of poetic justice and divine pity.

The *Corpus Juris* of Justinian, the perfected structure exhibited in the last Latin written in the Eastern Empire, was discovered to the west by Irnerius, who at the end of the eleventh century founded at Bologna the celebrated school of the Glossators. The new study spread like a forest fire through the newly-founded universities of Europe. Nay, more, it was often a cause of their foundation. It became, as Maine said, the *lingua franca* of jurisprudence. But for it the laws of Europe would be a chaotic confusion of local customs. By being incorporated, to a greater or less extent, in all the legal systems of the West the study of Justinian's code enabled centuries of legal development to be accomplished in a night, as it were. Except in England, Roman law is the concrete-bed of western civilisation, and Scotland and South Africa are two of the countries whose legal systems are securely based on it. The "Reception" of Roman law, as the humanised product of Roman character, was one of the greatest events in the history of modern civilisation.

It is the history, not the historians, of Rome which must count as the chief part of her legacy to the modern world. No Roman historian can be compared with Herodotus for vivid pictures of an ancient world surrounded by a strange, shadowy wonderland, or with Thucydides for the dispassionate analysis of political motives in peace and war, or even with Xenophon for the story of an epoch-making feat of arms.

It is true that the Roman historians are well worth reading for various reasons. The military histories of that great soldier and statesman, Julius Cæsar (102–44 B.C.), who was a master of direct narration, leaving his readers to follow the stern logic of circumstances, are models of a cold, calculated lucidity and have at first sight an appearance of disinterestedness, of impersonal truth-seeking. In the work " On the Civil War," which describes the way in which he attained autocracy, overthrowing his great rival, Pompey, the dramatic moments are not chronicled. We have to go to Plutarch (who wrote in Greek) for the famous story of the Rubicon and his proverbial exclamation, " The die is cast." But by degrees we become aware that these books are profoundly egotistical—that the history is made to tell throughout in favour of the generalissimo who was, in fact, describing his successful campaigns as an answer to his political critics. Sallust, again, though he has inklings of the scientific aspect of history, being in some measure a disciple of Thucydides, sometimes so distorts the facts as to cause his work to degenerate into a party pamphlet. His "War with Jugurtha," with its realistic descriptions of North Africa and exciting accounts of battles and sieges, is by far the best of his books, which were regarded by Martial, the maker of epigrams in verse, as the best Roman history that had ever been written, and were highly praised by Milton, that ripe Latinist. But Sallust has not the human interest of the honest, soldierly Xenophon, who knew the heart of the Greek citizen-soldier so well.

Livy (59 B.C.–A.D. 17) is a far more imposing figure in literature than either Cæsar or Sallust. His plan, which he carried out, was to recount the fortunes of the Roman people from their beginnings to his own times. Of his 142 "books," nearly a hundred, covering more than a hundred years, have been lost. Though Livy carefully consulted the available sources, earlier writers, family annals, public documents and oral traditions, he was not so much a great historian as a great man of letters. He can never resist a good story and all he asks of it is a fair degree of plausibility—for example, when relating how the Romans suddenly emerged from a mine and caught the King of Veii unawares while he was sacrificing, he excuses his credulity by saying, "In affairs so ancient I should be content if what looks like truth is taken as true." No Greek writer would ever have given himself away like that—not even Herodotus in his most guileless, garrulous moment! And Livy was not free from political prejudice, as may be judged from the good-humoured phrase "My Pompeian friend" applied to him by the Emperor Augustus who did not, however, resent the anti-Cæsarean colouring of his account of the Civil Wars. Again, even when he has trustworthy authorities before him, he is blind to their most admirable qualities. In his story of the Macedonian wars he follows Polybius obsequiously, but he is manifestly incapable of appreciating the great Greek historian's zeal for accuracy even in minute details and his statesmanlike judgment in questions of policy. He did not know enough of the art of warfare or of Roman law, and his accounts of campaigns and of great constitutional changes are often hopelessly confused. As to the "Patavinity" or provincial touch (he was born at Patavium, the modern Padua) imputed to him by Pollio, it is hardly apparent even to the most sensitive of modern scholars. But we can agree with the charge of negligence brought against him by the Emperor Caligula, who in such matters knew what he was talking about.

Livy, then, falls far below the standard of Thucydides and Polybius. For all that he is by far the greatest master of Augustan prose, and we can appreciate what the great critic Quintilian called "the indescribable eloquence" of the imaginary speeches in his narrative (he had adopted the Greek convention for summing up the arguments in great military or political controversies) and his pictures of famous personalities. His character of Hannibal, to take one of many examples, is one of the greatest things in ancient literature and quite unforgettable—I learnt it by heart in my schooldays and have remembered every word of it ever since. Whether it is true to life is another thing. Livy talks of Carthaginian treachery (*Punica fides*), and the transpontine theory of history, which makes one side all heroes and the other all villains and is the motive of much modern historical writing (see many Transatlantic histories of the relations of Great Britain and the United States), colours all he tells us of the struggle between Rome and Carthage, the most terrible of all ancient wars. If Livy had been a Greek, he would have been fair to the Carthaginians, who were certainly not more treacherous than the Romans or more ruthless in using a military advantage—just as

Thucydides was fair to the Spartans and Herodotus to the Persians. Yet he is in Latin prose what Virgil is in Latin poetry—the maker of a majestical prose-epic, full of almost Venetian colour and the glow of patriotism and the stir and clangour of tremendous events. If his knowledge of military science and art is inadequate, yet his battle-pieces—*e. g.* the description of the stricken field of Pydna where the Macedonian phalanx was destroyed by the more mobile and adaptable Roman legions—are amazing works of literary art. The noble line of the antique Roman poet, Ennius—

> "Moribus antiquis stet res Romana virisque,"

might have been the text of his history in which the old manners and the old heroes are glorified as the impregnable basis of Roman power, and the Republic, as it were, canonised. "Into no other commonwealth," he says, "were greed and luxury so long in entering; in those later days" (under the Empire) "avarice had grown with wealth, and the frantic quest of pleasure is rapidly leading to the ruin of the whole fabric of society; in our ever-accelerated downward course we have already reached a point where our vices and the cures for them are both intolerable." He thinks that Rome is going to the dogs, as our saying is, and this fallacy falsifies all the values in the picture of the centuries gone by. But to him, more than to all other authors, we owe our conception of the great statesmen and soldiers of the Republic, and these shadows of great names pass by in his *Historiæ ab Urbe Condita* as in a wondrous pageant, a triumph winding up the blue hills of Time to a timeless Capitol.

Tacitus, who shows us the intimate history of the first century of the Empire in a succession of lurid lightning-flashes out of a "tiger sky," is not a trustworthy historian. He lived, it is true, at the height of his times. Tradition makes him born at Interamna early in Nero's reign, and he had a distinguished official career under the three Flavian Emperors, rising to the dignity of the consulship in the short reign of Nerva when he was just past his fortieth year. During the reign of Domitian he wrote nothing, and the passage in his "Agricola" (the beautiful memoir of his distinguished father-in-law which he wrote in the year of Trajan's accession) in which he explains this long silence sets the note of his later history. Under Domitian the books of Stoics who opposed the spirit of a bloodthirsty autocracy had been burnt publicly in the Forum by the decree of lick-spittle senators, "thinking that in that fire they consumed the voice of the Roman people, their own freedom, and the conscience of mankind. . . . Great indeed are the proofs we have given of what we can bear. The ancient time saw the utmost bounds of freedom, we the limit of slavery; robbed by an inquisition of the common use of speech and hearing, we should have lost our very memories with our voices, if it were as much in our power to forget as to remain speechless. Now at last our breath has returned; yet it is in the nature of human weakness that remedies are slower than the diseases they affect, and genius and learning are more easily extinguished than recalled. Fifteen years have been taken out of our lives, while youth lapsed in silence into age;[1] and we are the miserable survivors, not only of those who have been taken away from us, but also of ourselves." The original passage is a splash of verbal vitriol, an exceedingly bitter indictment of the wrong donc to the living and to posterity alike by the suppression of intellectual freedom from political motives.

The thirty books of his "Annals" and "Histories" gave the complete history of the Empire for eighty years after the death of its creator. About one half of it is extant; the whole story of Caligula's reign is lost, and there are other lamentable gaps. What we have, however, is one of the most deeply impressive works of classical antiquity, whether we regard it as history or as literature. His impressions become obsessions with the understanding reader. His power

[1] While still a young man Tacitus had written a delightful book on Oratory "De Oratoribus" in which his final compressed and allusive style is anticipated.

of description is unique—his scenes are stamped out like medals, by a single stroke of an imagination with the might of a trip-hammer. His pictures of great episodes are indeed drama and painting and sculpture all in the fewest possible packed words. Once you have grasped the full meaning of the sombre, compressed Latin, you can never forget his army mutinies (to take examples from the "Annals"), the dismay of the mutineers at an eclipse of the moon, the visit to the battlefield in Germany where the white bones of Varus' legions lie bleaching, the fall of the frivolous consort of Claudius, the poisoning of Britannicus, the starry night of Nero's attempt to murder his mother—and (from the "Histories") the horrible sack of Cremona, worse than anything in the Thirty Years' War, and the wanderings of the deserted Emperor Vitellius through his empty, silent palace. His delineation of personalities is as intensely interesting; especially in the case of three Emperors—the morose, crafty and evasive Tiberius, the weak and pedantic Claudius controlled by his freedmen, any one of whom might "rule the Roman world for a day," and the strange, incalculable perverted Nero "enamoured of things incredible." We are shown the epoch of the Julio-Claudian Emperors, on which Romans under the settled government of Trajan looked back as on a long nightmare thronged with monsters in the guise of human beings, as a time of prodigies and superhuman crimes, of terrible men and even more terrible women. Is it all a legend or not? Tacitus, as we read him, convinces us that it is all dreadful reality—that each Emperor, each successive incarnation of the "Fortune of the City," publicly deified before his death, was of the order of the Titans. Caligula throws an arch of prodigious span across the Forum that he may cross, without descending amidst mere mortals, from his palace on the Palatine hill to sup with his fellow-god, Jupiter of the Capitol. The death of Nero was for years regarded as a wild rumour in the confines of the Empire—how could so monstrous and malignant a deity have vanished in the common dust? The reader's sense of the reality of this long "Terror" is deepened by the zigzag lightning flashes and thunderous rolling of the author's style, in comparison with which the most ominous passages in Carlyle's "French Revolution" or Thomson's "City of Dreadful Night" are feeble and tame lucubrations. And Tacitus, furthermore, is the greatest master of historical epigram that ever lived. "The unknown is always taken for something grand" (*omne ignotum pro magnifico*), "they make a wilderness and call it peace" (*solitudinem faciunt, pacem appellant*), "happy in the occasion of his death" (*felix opportunitate mortis*), and the solemn and beautiful "shadow of a great name" (*magni nominis umbra*) are sentences and phrases which are alive in literature to-day, being quoted continually.

There is one great central truth in all the judgments of this deeply-embittered mind. The period he shows us in retrospect was a revolutionary epoch, in which the great frontier armies, ruthless and barbarous owing to long contact with barbarians, left the Rhine and Danube unguarded and filled the homeland with blood and fire, even the Capital itself going up in flames from the torches of German troops. It seemed vital to save the Empire in the same sense of the term as we hear the Russian rulers of to-day talking of "saving the Revolution." In all ages the establishment of a new form of governance is attended by such terrible birth-pangs and by the emergence of sinister figures, such as Robespierre or Lenin or the Julio-Claudian Emperors and their satellites, Tigellinus and Sejanus and the rest, who ignore the elementary rules of justice and mercy, private or public. Tacitus, even if the bitterness of his soul and that dangerous gift of tense, telling phrase-making cause him to exaggerate, is right in emphasising the revolutionary aspect of a period which saw a life-and-death struggle between Napoleonism and sheer Anarchy, Bolshevism without even a theory behind it. The problem of the Roman Empire in gestation, like the problem of the French Revolution, is only just beginning to be solved—by the careful use of collected and collated evidence, a sifting of the veriest dust of circumstance, very little of which is to be found in the works of the Roman historians. During all these dreadful years for Rome, the storm-centre of revolutionary and counter-revolutionary movements, the provincial administration was carried on, wisely and well for the most part, by able permanent officials. The Emperors and their confidential advisers and agents had to save the whole administrative edifice from the attacks of hostile movements which seem to have made the Senate their citadel. The Emperor's friends, silent and indefatigable in their business of crushing conspiracies as soon as they were about to strike, were a species of Committee of Public Safety. It was the Emperor on whose conspicuous and imperilled head all the burden of hatred was concentrated, and we cannot trust any of the ancient verdicts—least of all the Tacitean characters of Tiberius and even Nero—on their personal attributes and motives. These were necessarily abnormal men; the fear of assassination, for which the murder of Julius Cæsar was a fatal precedent, was ever before their mind's eye, even their nearest and dearest were corruptible and corrupted, and the burden of responsibility was too vast to be borne. In such cases, as history shows, men lose their moral sense and behave like madmen, in their lust to grasp pleasures that drug their forebodings for a few moments. It was not until the Imperial system was firmly established and universally accepted, after these generations of storm and stress, that the " good " Emperors appear on the Roman world-stage.

It is to the history of Rome, then, rather than to the Roman historians, that we must look for object-lessons in the art of statesmanship which may be serviceable to-day. This history gives us the only complete picture mankind as yet possesses of the rise, culmination, decline and fall of an Empire which was not purely a product of brute-force (as were Assyria and the colossal creations of Mongol conquerors). The British Empire is a very different polity from the Roman : it is based upon representative institutions; it stands for equity where Rome stood for law; it is everything that Rome was not, everywhere where Rome could never be. Nevertheless the majestical drama of the rise of Rome from small, dubious beginnings to the overlordship of the world, civilised or capable of civilisation, has a special interest for us—for it was not the result of brilliant individual genius (as was the ephemeral Empire brought into being by Alexander the Great) but the outcome of the slow but sure expansion of racial energy. Virgil saw this great truth when he wrote his famous line—

" Tantæ molis erat Romanam condere gentem,"

seeing clearly as we do, from our far, far standpoint in time, that Rome's great and glorious achievement was the building-up of a *race*, not the constitution by conquest of a world-State. The story of the Roman Republic is ennobled by the deeds of commonplace men, the vast majority of them nameless, who could always subordinate self-interest to the welfare of the whole community. They would die for Rome; what was of far greater consequence, they would willingly live for Rome. St. Augustine saw in this spiritual strength, as he watched for the imminent destruction of the Roman power by the influx of barbarian hordes from without, a sufficient justification of Rome's world-empire. He pointed to the patriotism of the Roman private citizen who bore "toil, poverty, exile, bereavement, loss of limbs, and even of life, in the effort to enrich the public good." Such unselfish loyalty, he thought, must be imitated by those who wished to be worthy citizens of the City of God, shining fair and calm and far beyond the flaming walls of the earthly world. The Roman manly courage (*virtus*) was the basal quality of all the Christian's enduring virtues. And because Roman patriotism survived the loss of the far-reaching pomp of the colossal world-power, it was possible for the Fortress on its inspired hill to become a Cloister visible from the four ends of the earth.

Rome was never a predatory Power. Wars

were forced on her against her will, and undertaken only when some vital interest was involved. The best proof of this is that she "muddled through" her wars, as we have done, never being fully prepared for any crisis in foreign affairs because she was much more interested in domestic politics. The Romans were modest in the contemplation of their successful campaigns (which so often began with lost battles), attributing victory to the "Fortune of the City." Once the struggle began, they went on with it to the end; they would never make peace while a foot of the invader remained on the sacred Roman soil. They were always willing to learn from the enemy (*Fas est et ab hoste doceri*), and that was one reason why they were always victorious in the end. The legion, which combined weight with mobility, was not a Roman discovery, as may be guessed; it was the development, as the outcome of experience in the field, of the Greek model of military organisation. But it was Roman courage and tenacity which made it the magnificent instrument that broke the Macedonian phalanx and was never itself broken (though sometimes overpowered by superior numbers) until lance and bow took the place of sword and throwing-spear and the Gothic heavy cavalry destroyed the great army of the Emperor Valens at the Battle of Adrianople (378 A.D.). Though not a sea-faring race, the Romans built up a great sea-power, when it was necessary to do so, that Carthage might be beaten. It is not easy to see how Hannibal could have been defeated in the Second Punic War but for the fact that Rome had command of the sea, so that the great Carthaginian commander could only receive reinforcements by the long and difficult land route from his base in Spain. Rome knew well how to hold what she had won in war; not only by material means, but also by a policy which did not ask the assent of the conquered. She gripped her conquests with the great military roads, built to last for ever, which ran through all the Mediterranean lands, and by colonies which were garrisons of soldiers planted out on the land. "Divide and rule" (*divide et impera*) was the basal axiom of Roman policy which crushed out all factors of local union, even forbidding in Trajan's reign the formation of a fire brigade and persecuting the Christian Church as being an unsanctioned corporation. Rome ruthlessly trampled out the embers of armed resistance and would, if it seemed expedient, massacre a whole people—as Julius Cæsar did in Gaul—without the searchings of heart felt by the Athenians over similar examples of *real-politik* pressed to logical conclusions. A defeated general marched in the Roman victor's triumph and was taken down into the dismal dungeons of the Tullianum just as the procession came in sight of the Capitol—so that the moment of deepest humiliation for the vanquished might coincide with that of the wildest exultation of the victors. But Rome was never cruel for cruelty's sake and Virgil's boast that she existed—

> "Parcere subjectis et debellare superbos,"

was on the whole warranted by a humane treatment of conquered peoples, with whose religious cults and private customs she did not interfere.

The history of Republican Rome in its earlier stages certainly exhibits the growth of a people which could create and enjoy a reasoned liberty, had no great extremes of wealth and poverty, and was capable of self-discipline in a crisis. But the old problem set to the Athenians—can a democracy govern an empire?—had to be answered when, after the reduction of Carthage to the position of a vassal State, the whole sovereignty of the Hellenised East fell into Roman hands. Rome's Eastern policy was inspired by a sincere enthusiasm for Greek culture and a desire to act as the champion of order and help peaceful trading States such as Rhodes and Pergamus. But the sudden influx of vast wealth proved demoralising and created "big business" interests which exercised tremendous power. The Republican institutions could not adapt themselves to the functions of a world-Power, and in the century of confusion (from the Tribunate of Tiberius Gracchus in 133 B.C. to the definite establishment of the Empire by Octavian (Augustus) in 27 B.C.) which saw the fall of the Republic, the contest between the popular party and the senate representing the aristocracy (the "knights" or financial order took one side or the other, according to the direction in which their interests pulled them) was carried on by force of arms. Marius, who destroyed the huge Germanic armies that threatened the very existence of the Empire (omen of the dangers that lay in the darkness, outside the orbit of legionary force!) became the popular champion and, by substituting voluntary enlistment for the citizen levy, broke the ties that bound the legionary to the community of civilians. From that time on the dictator in domestic politics was the successful general with a professional army at his back. Sulla, Pompey, and finally Julius Cæsar, were in succession the Napoleonic dictators. And it was the last-named who laid the foundations of the Empire, after conquering Gaul and thereby removing the haunting fear of Gallic invasions, but was assassinated at the foot of Pompey's statue in the senate-house (44 B.C.) before he could pacify the East by force of arms. This murder was perhaps the most grievous blunder in history, for it removed the greatest practical intelligence Rome possessed and involved a prolongation of the death-pangs of the Republic. When the Roman Empire became the organisation for propagating the Christian faith, ordained for that very purpose as it seemed by the will of God, the political crime of Brutus and Cassius took on a darker colouring and appeared as the worst of human crimes. So it came about that these arch-assassins were placed by Dante in the lowest circle of his Inferno in company with Judas Iscariot.

The period in which the Imperial system had to prove its will-to-live has already been touched on. Then we come to the age of the Antonines and the long and splendid peace which was viewed in retrospect by future generations with yearning eyes. It was no "Golden Age" from our point of view—for it was only the well-to-do that were happy and serene in their Epicurean faith, the toilers being immured in the country labour-houses or *ergastula*, into which Apuleius gives us a dreadful glimpse. By degrees, however, the saying *Civis Romanus sum* came to connote a feeling of the essential equality of all men as men, and this sentiment evolved, even during the slow decline and swift dissolution of the Roman world-State, into a noble ideal that still lives on in the heart of man and may not for ever prove ineffectual. . . . In all the long centuries of Roman History there are object-lessons for the present, but they must be cautiously applied, with a full recognition of the differing circumstances, and must never be allowed, above all, to cause us to despair of the future.

In his latest novel,[1] which seems to be autobiographical so far as it touches on educational experiences, Mr. H. G. Wells makes his hero conceive a violent appetite for Latin. "For a few coppers," says Sarnac, relating his dream of life as he had lived it two thousand years before, "I bought in a second-hand bookshop an old and worn Latin *Principia* written by a namesake Smith; I attacked it with great determination and found this redoubtable language far more understandable, reasonable and straightforward than the elusive irritable French and the trampling coughing German I had hitherto attempted. This Latin was a dead language, a skeleton language plainly articulated; it never moved about and got away from one as a living language did." Though he repeats a stock fallacy of the opponents of an education based on Humanism in describing Latin as "a dead language, a skeleton language," Mr. Wells praises the straightforward reasonableness of Latin aright in this passage and suggests the explanation

[1] "The Dream," by H. G. Wells (Jonathan Cape, 1924).

why Latin, unlike the far more subtle and supple Greek, has been, and is likely to be, retained as one of the studies included in a liberal education. The study of Latin makes for clear thinking and the concise and coherent expression of thought, and for that reason alone would be an excellent training for any brain-worker.

But there are other advantages to be gained by learning Latin. It is a key to Italian, Spanish, Portuguese, Provençal, and French, which are the direct descendants of the *lingua rustica* or colloquial speech spoken throughout the Roman Empire in its later years. If you know Latin, it is much easier to acquire a real knowledge of any one of these derived languages, especially if you make yourself acquainted with the differences which rendered the *lingua rustica* more adaptable than classic or written Latin to the needs of ordinary life. The colloquial speech of the Roman citizen in Britain or Syria, in Sicily or Gaul, was never, it must be remembered, a means of rough-and-ready intercourse between peoples intellectually far apart (as is the "pidgin-English" used in the Far East) or a degenerate form of the Latin of educated persons (as the South African *Taal* is of Dutch). Nor was it a mere dialect, differing from that of cultured Rome as the vernacular of Somerset or Lancashire differs from the English of books and cultured people. It was a complete language, the one and only heiress of the Roman mother-tongue, which increased its vocabulary by taking in words from the languages of Romanised peoples (a process which has so greatly added to the resources of English) and by making good some of the deficiencies in classic Latin.

Secondly, Latin unlocks a vast treasury of literature, which includes not only the works of the ancient Roman poets and prose-writers, but also the chronicles and philosophies of the Middle Ages, and a vast amount of the "literature of knowledge," to use Matthew Arnold's phrase, produced during the later centuries when it was the accepted means of learned and diplomatic communications between all the peoples and languages of the Western World. Latin did not become a "dead language" when it ceased to be the medium of everyday conversation. In particular, it was always the official language, so to speak, of Christianity in the West—the language of its ritual, its scriptures, its books of education and of edification, its statecraft and its theology. Considering that Latin is the language of the Mass and of the Vulgate, we can dismiss the suggestion that it is "a dead language, a skeleton language," as based on a sad ignorance of modern civilisation. From end to end of Christendom to-day, without a moment's cessation during the twenty-four hours, the wonderful drama that concludes with the Latin words *Ite, missa est* is being enacted in the Roman churches (even in those subjected to the anti-Christian tyranny of the Russian Bolshevists) and millions of worshippers find in its ancient phrases an unfading splendour of musical imagery, a day-spring of eternal solace and inspiration. And St. Jerome's Latin translation of the Bible, which is commonly called the Vulgate, is even to this day one of the world's most widely-known and most profoundly inspiring books. It was undertaken by that mighty scholar, so vehement in controversy, because of a dream he had (so an old legend relates) in which Christ appeared to him and rebuked him for preferring to be a Ciceronian rather than a Christian. But St. Jerome's enthusiasm for the stateliest prose of Cicero was nobly expressed in his immortal translation which is full of solemn cadences (like those in Cicero's *Somnium Scipionis*—an imitation of the vision of Er in Plato's "Republic") which fall on the mind's ear like bell music pouring down from a belfry in the skies. All subsequent English literature has been influenced by our Authorised Version of the Book of books. But the Vulgate has had as deep an influence over a wider world for a far greater expanse of time. How ridiculous, then, to think of Latin as a "dead language," as though it were no more to us than "marble's language" for eighteenth-century epitaphs!—Latin that is the living voice of the great ages of Christianity and in a true sense the tongue and tocsin of eternity!

Thirdly, the Latin of the classical masterpieces is a treasury of word and phrase from which modern languages—even a tongue as alien and remote from the spirit of Latinity as Russian—have never ceased to draw additions to their own vocabularies. And the inner form, the patterns of thought and emotion, of the books bequeathed to us from ancient Rome have also from time to time profoundly affected several of the literatures of the modern world. In the eighteenth century, for example, it was seriously attempted to re-model English prose on Latin lines. Johnson and others consciously wrote in a "Ciceronian" style, and the example of Cicero as the first master of letter-writing, and perhaps the greatest of all, was sedulously followed by Horace Walpole, despite his "Gothic" sympathies and by Cowper and Gray, to name only these. This is but one of the innumerable instances of the kind which can be adduced from the critical study of the literatures of Western Europe. . . . So the truth is that the Latin language, bringing as it did with it the invaluable gift of the Roman alphabet,[1] is perhaps the most vital part of the legacy of ancient Rome to the modern world.

[1] The late Dr. Henry Bradley, in his erudite essay on *Language* in "The Legacy of Rome" (Oxford: Clarendon Press, 1923) says: "The Roman alphabet is not only the possession of the speakers of Neo-Latin, Germanic, and Gothic languages, but is used also by several of the Slavonic peoples, by the Hungarians and

The value and vitality of Latin having been thus demonstrated, it will be interesting to fill out the three arguments outlined above. It is impossible, of course, to do more than indicate a few main points which may help the reader to understand how much the modern world would have lost if Rome in her infancy had been crushed by the Etruscan power, with its mysterious language that is still meaningless to us, or had been overwhelmed at a later stage of growth by Carthage in the deadly struggle for supremacy in the Mediterranean. In either case there could have been no *lingua rustica* and four great languages and literatures—Italian, Spanish, Portuguese and French—would be non-existent to-day. It would be too wild an essay in the might-have-been to try to imagine what we should have got in place of them, if Etruscan or the Semitic language of the Carthaginians had been the tongue of the world-conquerors. Greek would perhaps have become the unchallenged world-language and the colloquial form of Greek (*koinē*), in which the Gospels were written, the basis of many modern languages.

I. The *lingua rustica*, as has been said, supplied certain deficiencies which rendered classical Latin

---

Finns, and by many thousands of natives of Asia and Africa who never heard the sound of any European tongue." This alphabet gains ground yearly and will perhaps become universal.

a bit stiff and inconvenient as a means of face-to-face conversation. For example, there is no exact equivalent for our " yes " in classical Latin, a very curious shortcoming which worried the early translators of Greek into Latin as much as it does a modern Fifth-form boy who is translating English into Latin. St. Jerome in the Vulgate got over the difficulty of translating a repeated Greek affirmative (in Matt. v, 37: " Let your communication be Yea, yea and Nay, nay ") by writing *Est, est* (It is, it is). The " rustic " or rather " common " Latin used *sic*, which became usual as a direct affirmative in the south, and so gave rise to the Italian and Spanish *si* and the Portuguese *sim*. In the country which is now France, however, the usual word for " yes " was *hoc* in the southern parts and *hoc* combined with *ille* in the north. The former became *oc* and the latter *oil* (*oui* in modern French). Hence the division of the French dialects into two great groups—the *Langue d'Oc* and the *Langue d'Oil*. Again, classical Latin, like the Russian of to-day, had no articles, and the common speech made good this inconvenient omission, so far as a definite article was concerned, by its use of *ille*, which appears obviously in all the Romance languages—except in Portuguese where the initial "l" has vanished—and in Roumanian (Roumania is the land of the " Roman Legion," the garrisons of the Empire along the Danube) is tacked on to the end of the noun, which has a pretty musical effect in talk. The indefinite article lacking was everywhere supplied by the numeral *unus*, used without the stress proper to its employment numerically. It is also interesting, and often entertaining, to watch the processes whereby the common colloquial language of the citizen of the later Roman Empire enlarged and enriched its vocabulary. In some cases, no doubt, the new word was really a very old one, which had dropped out of polite parlance, but survived on the lips of unlettered folk. Thus many words which are no longer used in English books or Parliamentary speeches are still in familiar use among the toilers of the much-remembering countryside. And what is frowned upon as being a scrap of American slang (*e. g.* "disgruntled") sometimes turns out to be a fine old English word of most honourable lineage. Some of the words in the *lingua rustica*, which have usurped the places of the classical Latin ones and passed on, like worn-down coins that can still be identified, have a quaint look of slanginess about them. Thus *testa*, a "pot," is used for "head" in all the modern Romance languages (French *tête*), and *gabata*, a "porringer," has become by a process of attrition the French word for "cheek" (*joue*). Such intrusions of undignified metaphorical words (most slang is imagery) remind one of the popular use of such words as "dial" (for "face") and "bread-basket" (for "belly"), and it may be that solemn poets and dignified prose-writers, writing in daughter-languages of English centuries hence, will use them without the least sense of their ancient accompaniment of chaffing and laughter. Among words, the low comedian of to-day is the high tragedian or court functionary of the day after to-morrow.

It is a life-long study to trace the development of the various Romance languages from the Latin of streets and fields, of merchants and soldiers and workers. Italian is, of course, the nearest of all in appearance to ancient Latin, which is largely due to the fact that a very large number of words have been brought in from the literary mother-tongue, only the terminations being altered. As a famous Italian scholar once said to me: "Italian has gone back to live with her mother." The great distinction between Latin and Italian is the latter's bewildering variety of diminutives and augmentatives, which carry various nice changes of significance, not easily grasped by the foreigner. Spanish and Portuguese, the close affinity of which has been disguised by the dropping-out in the latter language of *l* and *n* between vowels, come next in nearness to Latin. And furthest of all are the languages of France—the melodious Provençal, that has been revived as a literary language by Mistral and others, and the classic French which, even if it looks far less Latin-bred than the other Romance tongues, is yet the chief heiress to the spirit of Latinity. For the Englishman who wishes to have a really secure knowledge of any of these beautiful languages, so rich in literature, the learning of Latin is a necessity. Otherwise much of the beauty which is memorial must for ever escape him.

II. The use of classical Latin, not only in writing but also in speaking, was universal in the Middle Ages. This was a result of the conversion of the Roman Empire to Christianity, which gave rise to a learned class of official interpreters—a class. which in the end became the only learned one in existence and has, as a matter of fact, existed continuously down to the age in which we are living. The Latin of the clergy, which imitated pagan models as well as the older Christian masterpieces, such as the works of St. Augustine, maintained its purity astonishingly well, and the monastic writers were not unsuccessful in their efforts to keep out the barbarisms that were so numerous in the speech of the laity. As time went on, in the centuries of dark confusion which followed the downfall of Rome, new compounds were invented (always according to the traditional rules of formation) and old words acquired new meanings. But the language of the cloister always remained Latin in form and spirit for the thousand years during which the word *clericus* signified not only a person ordained to religious functions but also a man of learning. There are great and glorious things in the mediæval Latin literature, the study of which has been sadly neglected in our universities. The Latin hymns alone, in which rhyme is used, as in the familiar

> "Dies iræ, dies illa
> Solvet sæclum in favilla,"

would warrant a keener interest in this wonderful and resounding treasure-house of remembrance.

Again, the pupils in the monastic schools were taught to speak Latin, and in many monasteries the conversation between the denizens was generally, sometimes always, conducted in Latin. Latin was, as a result, spoken by court functionaries and diplomatists and, indeed, by all persons who wished to be regarded as educated and polished. It was not until the end of the seventeenth century that it ceased to be the language of international negotiations, French then taking its place. In Poland, among other countries where there is a commingling of difficult languages, every well-born person was expected to speak Latin fluently. In the immortal novels of Sienkiwiecz, the Walter Scott of Polish literature, the setting of which is the terrible wars between the Poles and the revolting Cossacks of the Ukraine or the Swedish invaders of the seventeenth century, all the knights and ladies know Latin, and Zagloba—that amazing compound of a Falstaff and a Ulysses—can make at need a long and polished oration in Ciceronian style. Russians and Swedes and Poles and Germans, not knowing one another's language, found Latin an indispensable means of communication. In the Polish Diet, which was such an ineffectual body, owing to the *liberum veto*, most of the speeches were made in Latin.

The rise of the Universities in the later Middle Ages, to which the Renaissance gave such a tremendous impetus, was accompanied by an intensified interest in the Latin language. All text-books were written in Latin, and the famous teachers lectured in Latin. Indeed a great cosmopolitan republic of learning came into being, in which Latin was the common medium of intercourse. Even in later times, when the national vernaculars were flourishing and producing literary masterpieces, Latin was the accepted vehicle of science and scholarship. Thus it was in Latin that the epoch-making discoveries of Newton and Harvey were set forth. And even to-day, when scientists have to lose so much of the time that might all be given to research in puzzling out the meaning of papers in a number of languages and the possibilities of *Esperanto* or some other artificial language as a labour-saving instrument are being discussed, there is a good deal to be said in favour of restoring Latin to its old position as an international medium of the "literature of Knowledge."

III. The Latinisation, to coin a term, of a modern language and literature is not a process to be encouraged. English in the first stages of its growth fortunately escaped this danger. The speech of Englishmen before the Norman Conquest was wholly unlike Latin—it could not possibly be looked upon by the learned as a debased and corrupt form of their ancient medium of communication, as was the case with the vernaculars derived from the *lingua rustica*—and the writers in Old English, such as King Alfred, who was the Father of English prose, seldom resorted to the introduction of Latin words. The Norman conquerors and thehorde of foreigners who followed them to England and flocked into the monasteries, put an end for a long time to the growth of a native literature. When English once more became the common tongue of earls and churls alike, a new literary English had to be created, and a great number of Latin words with their endings clipped off in French fashion were introduced. In Elizabethan times new words formed from the Latin were very numerous, and in the so-called Augustan age of English letters the same process was again far too prevalent. The Latin scholar's poem with "pendent rames" for "hanging branches" and so on, which is one of the pleasantest jests of Oliver Wendell Holmes, reduces to absurdity the idea of improving English by Latinising it. The gulf between many English masterpieces of prose and the language of plain folk, which is a weak point in English, is the result of past efforts to realise this foolish idea. Yet we must never forget that "our noble English," after all, owes its wondrous power and variety to being the offspring of a marriage, in a manner of speaking, between a Teutonic and a Latin medium.

I

THE art of the Romans, whether we look upon it as Hellenistic—that is, based on Greek models throughout—or as containing original elements, is very disappointing to the artist. It is in the portrait busts of the early Empire that Rome's claim to originality in statuary is most strongly recognised. The treatment of the body in Roman statues is almost always unsatisfying—indeed more often than not it represents, not merely an uninspiring convention, but the degeneracy of a convention. Yet the portrait heads are in many cases living and appealing presentations of Roman character, having the air of *gravitas* that distinguishes it racially, and we may legitimately regard them, for all that they were generally the work of artists of Greek origin, as the last term in a long tradition that began and was for long continued in the ancestral *imagines* or wax masks of the dead-and-gone members of great families. The "shoulder bust," which was the characteristic Roman type of portraiture in marble, enabled the sculptor, while suggesting the power and impressiveness of the whole body, to concentrate on the personality revealed in the features of the face and in the pose of the head. The modern equivalent is the quarter-length or half-length painting.

As regards architecture, again, modern criticism not only denies originality to the Romans, but also attempts to destroy the illusion of strength and magnificence which worked in the minds of the mediæval builders who contemplated the gigantic relics of Roman civilisation. We can see, having entered into the Greek spirit, that Greek architects of the Periclean period would have found in the best Roman buildings a self-conscious straining after display (such indeed as is felt by a visitor to Berlin, still the ostentatious symbol of German Imperialism and likely to remain so to the end) which is repugnant to true art. The arch and the dome, which were once supposed to be Roman inventions, are now known to have been introduced to the notice of Greek builders as an outcome of the conquests of Alexander the Great. The Roman use of the arch was once thought to have been derived from the mysterious Etruscans, but that theory was demolished by the discovery that the great arched drain of Rome, the *Cloaca Maxima*, did not date from the days of the half-legendary Tarquins, but had been constructed during the Republican period. Greek architects were acquainted with the arch, though they preferred the beam, adhering with characteristic simplicity to a style of construction universal when houses were built of timber. The older Alexandria, the new capital built by Alexander in Egypt, perished utterly, but there is evidence extant to prove that it was a domed and vaulted city. And the earliest cupola in Europe is over a bath at Pompeii, which derived its art from the later Alexandria, not from Rome. It is impossible, then, to regard the Roman architecture as an original product of Roman genius. And when we examine such famous relics of Roman architectural grandeur as the Pantheon, built by Hadrian to the gods and goddesses of the seven planets, the truth which is the source of beauty in Greek art cannot be found in them. Looking at the outside of the Pantheon we see what seems to be a wall of solid brick-work (originally encased in marble) in which tiers and arcades of brick arches are so arranged as to bear up the vast weight of the entire edifice. Actually, these brick arches are a fraud; the brick-work is a mere casing, a few inches thick, which hides the 20 ft. thick wall of solid concrete which really does the work. The Romans invented concrete, which enabled them to build rapidly and cheaply on a huge scale, and they had a way of veiling this cheapness by a variety of devices, which, to use their own phrase, were *splendide mendax* (magnificently untruthful). It is from the Romans that the modern world derives its universal custom, which would have been deeply disgusting to the Greek lover of artistic truthfulness, of concealing the plain serviceableness of ordinary buildings by a redundancy of deceptions that are supposed to be decorative. It is a sad pity that the impressiveness of the Pantheon's interior should be marred by the after-thought of an exterior sham. As engineers the Romans were marvellous; as architects, they were sadly to seek, the differences between the Parthenon and the Pantheon measuring their decline from the ideal of Greek art. After all, there is a more unmixed satisfaction to be found in their cranes for building or water-clocks or the taxi-cab arrangement for measuring the distance travelled by a hired vehicle (the two latter described by Vitruvius) than in their architectural prodigies. For in the case of these contrivances serviceableness was fully attained and freely confessed; there was nothing sham or shame-faced about them.

In Latin literature, however, which bridges the abysm of time between Ennius and Erasmus, we possess a legacy of Roman art which expresses the inner spirit of the race. The moulds of literary art, it is true, are all of Greek invention. But the Roman poets and prose-writers poured new wine into these old bottles; in this domain at any rate the Roman mind did not merely adopt and adapt, but was constructive and creative. Latin is the second mother-tongue of our civilisation and the literary masterpieces in that stately medium are nearer and dearer to us, by virtue of a longer and more intimate acquaintance, than the more beautiful, but more remote and austere creations of the Greek spirit. The language of ancient Greece will always, in all probability, remain a study for specialists; even if the reaction against the abolition of a "classical education" should prevent the modern world from returning to the warning of Greekless mediæval teachers when their pupils came upon a word or two of Greek in a Latin text: *Græcum est, non legitur* ("It's Greek, so we skip it"). "The civilisation of Greece, including its literature as well as its thought and art," writes Dr. J. W. Mackail,[1] who is the most illuminating of living guides to Latin Literature, "is a stimulant which, taken undiluted, is an intoxicant. The liberating power which has been justly claimed for it is often like the liberation of a high explosive. For use, it has to be brought under control; to become a fructifying force, it had to be interpreted and recast by another civilisation, that of Rome. . . . It is largely through Latin, and still more through the Latinised mind which we have inherited, that the Greek sources have to be approached and Greek thought transformed (to

* In the essay on *Literature* in "The Legacy of Rome" (Oxford: Clarendon Press, 1923), edited by Mr. Cyril Bailey.

use a metaphor from science) into the voltage for which the mechanism of our own minds, and of the world we live in, is fitted."

II

The Romans themselves, looking back on the achievements of their race, placed the beginnings of their literature in the twenty years of peace following the First Punic War. The position of Rome in the Mediterranean sun had been secured, and those who had leisure and wealth and the open-mindedness that comes therefrom, set about enlarging the narrow culture of the land-locked State which had been forced, against its will, to enter on a great overseas adventure and had acquired the rich islands of Sicily and Sardinia as the rewards of victory. They rightly felt that a "Great Power," with footholds in the great international inland sea, must be at any rate able to understand the mentality of its potential friends—*i. e.* the Hellenised States which were also opposed, ethically and ethnologically, to the Carthaginian polity. Naturally, necessarily, the new Latin literature, which was an outcome of this inevitable impulse, began with translation of Greek epic and dramatic poetry. Thus a translation of the "Odyssey" into Saturnian verse (an indigenous verse-form of which the nursery line—

"The Queen was in her parlour | eating bread and honey,"

is an excellent example) was made by Andronicus, a Greek prisoner of war from Tarentum, who acted as tutor to the children of the ruling classes at Rome. In his dramatic pieces, which included both tragedies and comedies, Andronicus kept to the Greek metres, and the Latin playwrights who followed him, such as Nævius, who was the first Latin poet of consequence, followed his example. All these earlier men wrote comedies as well as tragedies of the kind known as *palliata* or "robed in the Greek mantle" (Milton's "sweeping pall"), being translations or adaptations of Greek originals. In addition to these there was the comedy called *togata*, or "dressed in Roman style," of indigenous manners, customs, and types, of which only a few small fragments are extant.

It is not necessary for my purpose to examine the scant relics of the works of these pioneers. The *fabula togata*, though Lucius Afranus wrote comedies of manners that were compared with Menander's, died out because the great majority of Romans—the dole-supported mob and the young man about town with his mistress—preferred the evolutions of naked dancers and the battles of gladiators to the delicate wit and humour of true comedy. Tragedies, again, such as held the attention of the assemblage in the theatre of Dionysus at Athens were not strong meat enough for a population used to the bloody spectacles of the Colosseum, in which they themselves were the arbiters of life and death, expressing their will by a movement of the thumb. Adaptations from the New Comedy of Athens (directly comparable with our adaptations from the French) were popular, and we happen to possess in a fairly complete form the works of Plautus and Terence, two of the most successful purveyors of these derived plays. Plautus (born 254 B.C.) has been, by the irony of circumstances, the sole representative for future ages of the lost examples, a vast volume, of the Athenian comedy of life as it is lived. He has been one of the most persistent influences in the history of the world's literature; among his innumerable disciples Molière is the most famous, though he could not improve on the ease and vivacity of his ancient master's dialogue or even on his characterisation and stagecraft. No doubt Plautus owed much of the ingenuity shown in construction to Menander and his other Greek models. The twenty plays of Plautus that are extant include specimens of every type of play to which the term comedy can be applied. Too many of them are concerned with the environment of bawds and harlots, but the coarseness of his frank essays in pornography lack that dangerous intriguing subtlety which is the worst feature of our Restoration drama. It is almost all "cleanly wantonness," in Herrick's phrase. Sometimes the chief motive, sometimes the principal character, in these plays has made them remarkable in themselves and helpful to modern dramatists. Thus the "Menæchmi" presents for the first time the famous device of the twin-brothers who had not met since their childhood and by their close resemblance give rise to all manner of comical confusions in the town they visit together, when old enough for fighting and loving. But for this inexhaustible invention Shakespeare's "Comedy of Errors" might never have existed. On the other hand, the "Aulularia" or "Pot of Gold" is just a setting for the living and breathing portrait of the old miser, Euclio—who is the original of Molière's Harpagon. My own favourite is the "Rudens" ("The Rope"), a romantic comedy which has for the speaker of its prologue the star Arcturus, develops its plot between sunshine and sea-sheen on a rocky beach near Cyrene, and recalls both "The Tempest" and "The Winter's Tale" of our arch-dramatist, who derived so much, directly and indirectly, from the Plautine comedy. A true dramatist, having also an unerring sense of the theatre, Plautus has been as far-reaching an influence in his special sphere as Cicero has been in the making of prose style.

He was not, however, "literary" in the sense that Terence was. Terence, who was born soon after the ruin of the Carthaginian power at Zama, reached Rome as a boy-slave, and was bought, educated, and manumitted by a wealthy senator who recognised his unusual gift for literature. He became the pet of a literary coterie, the friends of the younger Scipio Africanus, who were a sort of academy for the refining of the Latin language. Thus was evolved what Julius Cæsar, as able in literary criticism as in his larger activities, called a "half Menander"—a writer of polite comedy in polished Latin, which set a standard of urbanity to his own and to all later ages. There is no "punch" in the Terentian drama, but the charm of the brilliant Congreve-like dialogue and the delicate portraiture, and an occasional line in the patronising prologues such as the immortal—

"Homo sum: humani nihil a me alienum puto,"

have made it a great formative influence in literary drama and still entrances the scholar who can appreciate the nice shades of the unruffled diction.

Terence must have seemed to the spectacle-loving citizens of Rome a high-brow, superior-minded dramatist. One of his six extant plays was twice a dead failure; on the first presentation, if we are to believe the prologue written for the third performance, because "that ass, the public," was excited about a tight-rope exhibition that was to follow the play; on the second, because everybody left the theatre owing to a rumour that gladiators were to be on view elsewhere. After the death of Terence the only forms of the drama which were popular at Rome were the Mimes and Atellane plays, the latter farces which were liked because the audience could read into them satirical allusions to high-placed persons. Caligula burned an author alive in the arena who had made a joke in one of these farces which could be construed as a hit at himself, Jupiter's own brother. The query of Augustus on his death-bed when he asked his friends if he had played the " mime " of life (not the " comedy ") to their satisfaction shows how sketches from everyday life, seasoned with coarse immorality and wisdom in tabloid form, retained their popularity. The tragedies of Seneca (born about the beginning of the Christian era) were closet dramas and, furthermore, plays with a moral purpose. It is impossible to believe that a Roman audience could have tolerated his declamation and psychological hair-splittings, which take the place of action and emotion. But the popular taste would not have been offended—rather it would have been intensely gratified—by such un-Greek horrors as the sight of Theseus in the " Phædra " piecing together the fragments of his son's mangled body, or the terrific outbursts of ranting which occur at a crisis. Now and again Seneca hits upon a good piece of business as when, in his "Troades," Ulysses comes to fetch Hector's son, Astyanax, for execution, and Andromache, who has hidden the child in his father's tomb, can truthfully assert that he is with the dead, gone from the light of day. Ulysses, rejoicing that the possible avenger of Troy is no more, hurries off in delight, then stops and remembers that he has only a parent's word for the fact. Observing the Queen closely, he suspects it is fear, not grief, that afflicts her; and with his traditional cunning, says that she is happy in that her son has escaped the terrible death designed for him, to be flung from the last tower of Troy left standing. Andromache cannot repress a start, a word of horror. So by degrees he picks up the scent, as it were, and eventually sets his men to pull down Hector's tomb, whereupon the poor mother, afraid that her child will be crushed in the ruin of the massive monument, reveals his hiding-place. All this was hugely admired by Seneca's many modern imitators. Indeed his tragedies have had a tremendous influence, not only with our Elizabethan dramatists, but also with Corneille, Racine and even Alfieri. There seems to be no possible doubt if literary style be a sufficient criticism, that these tragedies were the work of the philosopher and statesman who was entrusted by Agrippina with the education of Nero, shared the administration of the Empire with Burrus, the Captain of the Guard, and so laid the foundation of his colossal fortune and in the end received from his terrible pupil the order to commit suicide, which he obeyed with courage and dignity. His so-called "Dialogues," which are written in the vocabulary of ordinary cultured conversation, are so full of epigrams that Montaigne complained they made it difficult to read much of them at a sitting. But these epigrams are evolved naturally, are not forced.—"If Seneca sparkles," said Diderot, "it is as the diamond sparkles or the star, because it is his nature." Even when Ciceronianism became the overruling fashion, writers of all nations drew liberally upon the great store-house of Senecan wit and wisdom, and his influence as a sort of universal-provider of moral reflections and aphorisms reached its climax in England during the first half of the eighteenth century. Pope's "Essay on Man" is Senecan through and through, both in manner and matter.

III

Cicero, however, is by far the greatest and most influential of Roman prose-writers. The Roman historians, with whom I have dealt in a previous chapter, cannot compare with him, jointly or severally, as a formative factor in the literature of the world. Indeed he was in prose what Virgil was in poetry—a bridge leaping in a single unbroken span from the ancient to the modern world. Not only the customary prose of the Roman Empire, but also that of St. Jerome and St. Augustine, of the mediæval Church, and of the earlier and later Renaissance was Ciceronian. Even to-day the Sixth-form boy or the writer of a Latin epitaph tries to use Cicero's vocabulary in the way Cicero used it. Cicero was not a great original thinker, but he devised a supple and sumptuous prose, a really wonderfully complete instrument of expression, which also propagates an atmosphere of *humanitas*, as a flower its perfume, and so fosters and ennobles the sense of Græco-Roman culture. Time was when Cicero's reputation tyrannised over the minds of the Renaissance—when he was regarded as the equal of the great Greek philosophers in ethics and metaphysics and the peer in oratory of Demosthenes. In later centuries his copiousness came to be distrusted; he was sneered at as a "mere journalist," as one who substituted phrase-making for thinking and feeling. To-day we admit, while insisting that Cicero was neither a philosopher nor a statesman of the first rank, that Ciceronianism has always been one of the vital forces of world-culture.

As a forensic orator he has never been surpassed. His speeches as chief counsel for the prosecution of Verres for maladministration in the government of Sicily were never excelled, even by himself, in richness of style, ease and lucidity, and the power of making effective use of vast masses of evidence. This prosecution was political, an attack on the Sullan constitution, and Cicero's conspicuous success made him the chief orator in the Pompeian party. His defence of Aulus Cluentius Habitus on a charge of poisoning, which is a dazzling flash-light on the social life of Rome and the provincial towns, and the "Pro Archia" uttered in defence of a Greek man of letters, who was a member of his literary circle and a personal friend, are noble examples of Ciceronian eloquence, permanent treasures of Latin literature. In all such orations Cicero is addressing not only the forum, but the whole civilised world, for he has the gift of lifting a case and a cause above the plane of judicial problems and exhibiting it as a lesson for humanity in the strength and weakness of human nature. His later speeches, including his fourteen "Philippics" against Antonius, are not quite so splendid in their sonorous actuality, for his personality was becoming more and more engrossed in those philosophic masterpieces, of which the "De Oratore" and the delightful "De Senectute" and "De Amicitia" (quarries for all the essayists and makers of imaginary dialogues that have ever lived) are among the most finished examples.

It is in such minor works as the "Somnium Scipionis" that we hear most clearly the organ music of the Ciceronian style in its noblest form, the solemn cadences of which have passed into the Vulgate and the liturgy of the Church of Rome. His poems, which may have revealed him as the Kipling of his age, building stately fugues on such resounding phrases as *Fortuna Populi Romani* (Dr. J. W. Mackail poetically compares them to a bourdon stop in the oration "Pro Lege Manilia"), have unfortunately been lost. His letters, happily, are extant, and in the collection preserved and edited by his secretary, Tiro, the "Epistolæ ad Familiares," a large number of those addressed to him by various compatriots are to be read. As a letter-writer Cicero has a vivid, easy, even slip-shod style in which the gossip of his times is colloquially presented—indeed, as we read we seem to be listening to the after-dinner talk of the social personages of the Rome he knew and loved so well.

Latin literature is none too rich in these revelations of social life. In later ages than Cicero's, however, Petronius Arbiter—in all probability the same person who was Nero's *arbiter elegantiarum* or master of the ceremonies—gave us a humorous character-sketch of the newly-rich Trimalchio, and Apuleius opened for a moment the gates of the gloomy *ergastula* or labour-houses in which the toilers of the Imperial world-State dragged out their joyless existence. These two writers were the pioneers of the picaresque novel, to whom Cervantes and other modern masters owe a great deal.

IV

Ennius was the first of the great Roman poets, and the most Roman of them all. He was a busy writer, perhaps the first professional man of letters in the Western world, and until his death at the age of seventy he was hard at work producing treatises on all sorts of literary subjects. But his fame rests on his tragedies (often quoted by Cicero, who greatly admired his work) and the epic "Annales" in which he related the history of the Roman power from the fabulous arrival of Æneas in Latium down to his own days. He adapted the hexameter to his purpose, which was to glorify the proud virtue and the very narrow, but very strong, character of the makers of the Republic. There are such a rugged force and truthfulness in the few hundred lines of the "Annales" which have come down to us, and such a broad and unfaltering sagacity, that we are not surprised that he was for a whole century (until the appearance of Virgil's epic, in fact) regarded as almost the Homer of the Roman race. Such weighty and memorable lines as—

"Quem nemo ferro potuit superare nec auro"

and the fine simile of that judicious critic, Quintilian, who likens his epic to a holy grove of aged oaks, filling the observer's soul with solemn awe rather than with the delight inspired by sheer beauty, cause us to look upon the loss of his works as one of the great literary catastrophes.

A still greater poet, ranked by some of the Augustan critics above Virgil, nearly met a similar fate. All the manuscripts of the amazing "De Rerum Natura" of Lucretius (born 94 B.C.) are copies of a single original, and if that had perished, we should have known nothing of one of the greatest poets and philosophers of antiquity, so few are the allusions to the man and his work in Latin literature. Both as literary achievement and as scientific prophecy the work of Lucretius is unique; he might be compared with Milton, not only for his powerful technique and lofty moral, but also for his aloofness from the literary movements of his day, the chief of which originated in the Alexandrian clearing-house of ideas. Homer and Euripides are the only poets Lucretius mentions; truth, not beauty, was the object of his high quest, but though he never faltered in his long journeyings to seek the ultimate secrets of the universe he finds all manner of beautiful and poignant things by the wayside. The Lucretian hexameter is a simpler and mightier thing than Virgil's; it has the mass and momentum of things and actions and is a development of the Ennian line, having more variety yet no less power. His Latin, moreover, is the pure and perfect idiom, owing nothing to alien sources, such as is found nowhere else save in the *pura et inlustris brevitas* of Cæsar at his best.

Epicureanism was a religion, not merely a philosophy, with Lucretius, and his great purpose was to cure mankind of that fear of death, and of what might follow it, which makes human life so anxious and despicable. To the true Epicurean death was not to be feared at all, for longing does not survive it and nothing whatsoever happens after it. It is a perfect and everlasting Nirvana, an eternal sleep with never a dream. But it is his vivid anticipations of the scientific discoveries of to-day—the constitution of the atom, the nature of light, the beginnings of human society as seen by the imagination—which most amaze the modern world and have given him a place in the hierarchy of creative thinkers who can transcend the horizons of their age and their ego.

We wonder at Lucretius, but we love Virgil, who can wring our hearts, as he wrung the hearts of Rome, with the sense of tears—the "tears of things" in the most magical of all his lines—

> "Sunt lacrimæ rerum et mentem mortalia tangunt"—

behind all the sustained splendours of his golden verse. There are times when we think of him, as we think of Sophocles or of our own Tennyson, as greater in his artistry than in his love of the truth whereof beauty, at least the lesser beauty, is but a fleeting shadow. Now and again we are conscious of a fastidiousness which gilds that which is golden. We know him to have been the most fastidious of master-poets. On his death-bed he besought that the "Æneid" might be destroyed, on the score that it required three years of further work to perfect it. The Emperor's command (which alone should wash away all his faults in the world's undying gratitude) prevented this wish from being carried out. It is dreadful to think what mankind would have lost if this day-spring of all romanticism had remained unknown to the sequent ages. Virgil *is* the Roman Homer—for the old foolish idea that the "Iliad" and the "Odyssey" are "natural" epics, whereas the "Æneid" is "artificial," has long been confuted by the new knowledge of history which shows the Homeric age as a late term in a long series of steps towards a civilisation complete in itself. Homer is as consciously artistic as Virgil; more so, perhaps, in his characterisation and in his management of episodes But there is nothing so modern in the Homeric poems as the wonderful portrait of Dido, which may have been suggested by the Medea of Apollonius—if he stole, Virgil knew what to do with the stealings, which is a mark of the triumphant artist in every age. It is the sad earnestness, the secret compassion of Virgil which made him the chief poet of the Middle Ages, being in the eyes of Christians a soul that was by nature Christian, and caused him to be Dante's guide through a more dreadful underworld than that of the greatest book of his "Æneid."

Horace is the man of the world in poetry; in his work we are conscious of the *curiosa felicitas* ("careful happiness"—the blest inevitableness that comes of taking infinite pains), yet cannot understand why he is the most popular of Latin poets. He is half-way between Herrick and Pope, both of whom lacked inspiration: without the flower-like freshness of the former or the Senecan sententiousness of the latter. Gautier is perhaps the nearest parallel to him in modern literature; like Horace, he gave us carven gems and his conviction that "the work emerges more beautiful" if the medium be hard to handle, the least slip being fatal, would have been shared by the Roman master-craftsman. The art of Horace is nearer akin, surely, to sculpture than to music. And the quality of urbanity, which almost makes a gentleman of this world a man for the next, is manifest in him in its ripe perfection. Neither God nor the Good Devil, one feels, could ever be angry with Horace, and he for his part would never lose his temper, much less his temperament. Where Virgil, his contemporary, is august, Horace remains impeccably, irresistibly Augustan.

Yet if the "lyric cry"—the word that is a pang—be vital to lyrical poetry, then Horace was not of the order of singers in which we read the names of Sappho, of Burns, of Shelley, of Heine, and of how few others! Catullus, however, is surely of that blest-unblest company. In all literature there is nothing to surpass in fire and tears, in the passion that is as much loathing as loving, the lyrics which Catullus addressed to his Lady of Lesbos, the absolute mistress of his heart, yes, and his brain. She was one of those *grandes amoureuses*, no doubt, about whose graves the corpse-light of scandal flickers for ever—yet, since they can make poets and men of action out of mere clogs of flesh, they are in their way benefactors to the human race. Clodia, for such was the real name of the Lesbia of these intolerable love-poems, these insatiable songs of hate, was a Claudian by birth and the wife of Cecilius Metellus, so that she was by birth and marriage linked to the proudest of aristocratic families. Cicero in a petulant moment (perhaps she had patronised that vain and loquacious "plebeian" a little) sneers at her great blazing eyes, and the chroniclers do not forget to tell us that she was seven years older than Catullus, as if that mattered at all. The woman amorist is never older or younger than her vocation. The lyrics of Catullus are a fugue of piercing music on the famous lines:—

"Odi et amo: quare id faciam fortasse requiris;
Nescio, sed fieri sentio et excrucior."

(I hate and love: you ask how that can be;
I know not, but 'tis agony to me.)

The first rapture turning all fleshly things into a white leaping flame, passes away; but the desire of the flesh abides and the enthralment. Wrongs only cause the fire to blaze up afresh; there are raptures and reconciliations; yet his hatred for this Circe-like enchantress waxes continually. Perhaps, if there had been no Clodia for him, he would have been as great a lyric poet in a happier mode, for his "Ode to Diana," short as it is, is a masterpiece, and his Epithalamium for Mallius and Vinia is full of future chimes and has a richness of imagery which challenges the Song of Solomon or the Ode of Sappho I have commented on in a previous chapter. Yet it had been a loss to the world for all time if we had missed his story of a grand passion which begins with love's defiance of age and wisdom, out-kisses the number of sands and stars, and ends in such rancour and repining that the last farewell is a gross insult by proxy—and little the lady cared about it, having taken in her toils another brilliant and erratic young aristocrat.

There is a fading, a falling off, as we cross over into the age of "Silver Latin," of the autocrat of taste, of language with "point," of the salons and of the declamations. Pope presided over a similar age in the history of English literature.

Yet in the master-versifiers of this age—Martial, Juvenal, Lucan—we have writers who have never ceased to be cunningly imitated by the moderns. It is society, not humanity, with which they are mainly concerned. Martial with his 1,200 epigrams "seasoned with true Roman wit," as he himself boasts (and indeed he owes little to the Greeks, whose conception of the epigram was very different) holds his distorting mirror up to all the possible and impossible types of social bipeds that infest a great city. These very types are always with us, and there is not one of Martial's successful epigrams, having a sting that stung, which has not been imitated again and again in modern times. Juvenal, the professional satirist, has many faults; worst of all, he did not, he dared not, attack the living. But his fierce indignation (*sæva indignatio*), which is only surpassed by Swift's, carries them all off in a flood of passionate eloquence. He has left us a cinematograph of the every-day life of Imperial Rome, and some of his oft-quoted lines are effectual even in English, when the force of his almost Lucretian hexameter is lost. Lucan, who took part in the Piso conspiracy against Nero and committed suicide at the age of twenty-six, wrote a modern epic, the "Pharsalia," which has, I think, been most unfairly belittled. It may be that the personages of the drama—Cæsar, Pompey, and Cato, who is the hero—are lay-figures, and that the fierce republicanism of the author is a sham, since it goes with abject flattery of the reigning Emperor. But it is a wonderful achievement for a mere boy, and some of its great lines, such as—

> " Nil actum credens dum quid superesset agendum "

written of Julius Cæsar, and

> " Victrix causa deis placuit, sed victa Catoni "—

are trumpet-clangs, which ring out across the ages, and the whole vast poem sustains its lofty note and stir of action in a marvellous fashion. What would Lucan have done had he lived long enough for so great a gift to ripen?

* * * * *

These are but a few of the Latin authors who have a message for us even to-day. As time goes on, and the tides of life in the great Empire slacken, the primal inspiration of Latin literature fails—but the Latin remains! There was not a day before the dreadful day when the city was taken and sacked by Alaric's army of Goths and Huns at which there existed no Latin poet or prose-writer who is not still worthy of close study. And now and again, as in the " Pervigilium Veneris " with its haunting refrain—

> " Cras amet qui nunquam amavit quique amavit cras amet "—

we have dulcet-clear anticipatory echoes of the songs that were to be sung in Provençal vineyards or in English meadows a thousand years later.

A Brief Bibliography

THOSE who wish to fill out the outline given in this little book should, in the first place, procure "The Claim of Antiquity" (Oxford Univ. Press, 1s. net), which contains a complete list of the best translations of Greek and Latin authors and books on the classics suitable for the general reader. The chief series of inexpensive translations are (1) Oxford Library of Translations (Oxford Univ. Press), (2) Everyman Library (J. M. Dent), and (3) World's Classics (Oxford Univ. Press). The Loeb Classical Library (Heinemann), which prints the Latin or Greek text with the translation opposite it, can be recommended to those who have the courage to try to read the originals. The reading of good translations, verse as well as prose, should be made the basis of all further study. The student should at the same time read "The Legacy of the Ancient World" (Macdonald and Evans), by W. G. de Burgh, M.A., Professor of Philosophy in University College, Reading, which is the only continuous and complete history in our language of the Jewish, Greek and Roman cultures, their complex relationships and their influence on mediæval and modern civilisation. The "Bibliographical Index" to this invaluable work will be most helpful to the more advanced student.

The following works can also be warmly recommended :—

(1) "The Legacy of Greece." A collection of Essays on the chief aspects of Greek culture by a number of leading authorities. Edited by R. W. Livingstone. Oxford Univ. Press.
(2) "The Pageant of Greece." A selection of translated excerpts from the great Greek writers suitably introduced and interpreted. Edited by R. W. Livingstone. Oxford Univ. Press.
(3) "Ancient Greek Literature." By Gilbert Murray. Heinemann.

(4) "Greece." By C. A. Fyffe. Macmillan. Though out of date for prehistoric Greece, as a result of the Cretan discoveries and for other reasons, this little primer is a masterly survey of Greek history and still the best introduction to the study thereof.

(5) "Ancient Times." By J. H. Breasted. Ginn and Co.

(6) "Science and Mathematics in Classical Antiquity." By J. L. Heilberg. Oxford Univ. Press.

(7) "The Legacy of Rome." Essays on the various aspects of Roman civilisation by a number of high authorities. Edited by Cyril Bailey. With an Introduction by the Right Hon. H. H. Asquith. Oxford Univ. Press. As reliable, if not as readable, as "The Legacy of Greece."

(8) "Latin Literature." By J. W. Mackail. Murray.

(9) "The Silver Age of Latin Literature." By Professor W. C. Summers. Methuen.

(10) "The Roman Empire." By H. Stuart Jones. (Story of the Nations.)

For the history of Greece and Rome, the ancient historians should be read (with a note-book) in good translations *pari passu* with modern writers, of whom a wide choice will be found in almost any free library. Gibbon's "Decline and Fall" is indispensable; it should be read in the edition with notes by Professor J. B. Bury, whose "History of Greece" is the best modern text-book on its subject. Mommsen's "History of Rome" is the most sympathetic history of its kind. The works of Zeller and Burnet on Greek philosophy, of Haig on the Attic Theatre, of Warde Fowler and Dill on Social Life at Rome, and of Maine on Ancient Law should be studied, and Bryce's "Holy Roman Empire" is indispensable for an understanding of the persistence of the Roman tradition through the Middle Ages.